Racialism and the Media

Rochelle Brock and Cynthia Dillard
Executive Editors

Vol. 114

The Black Studies and Critical Thinking series
is part of the Peter Lang Education list.
Every volume is peer reviewed and meets
the highest quality standards for content and production.

PETER LANG
New York • Bern • Berlin
Brussels • Vienna • Oxford • Warsaw

Venise T. Berry

Racialism and the Media

Black Jesus, Black Twitter,
and the First Black
American President

PETER LANG
New York • Bern • Berlin
Brussels • Vienna • Oxford • Warsaw

Library of Congress Cataloging-in-Publication Data
Names: Berry, Venise T., author.
Title: Racialism and the media: Black Jesus, Black Twitter, and the
first Black American president / Venise T. Berry.
Description: New York: Peter Lang Publishing, 2020.
Series: Black studies and critical thinking, vol. 114 | ISSN 1947-5985
Includes bibliographical references and index.
Identifiers: LCCN 2019033891 | ISBN 978-1-4331-7289-2 (hardback: alk. paper)
ISBN 978-1-4331-7288-5 (paperback: alk. paper) | ISBN 978-1-4331-7290-8 (ebook pdf)
ISBN 978-1-4331-7291-5 (epub) | ISBN 978-1-4331-7292-2 (mobi)
Subjects: LCSH: African Americans and mass media. | Race in mass media. |
Race relations in mass media. | Mass media and race relations—
United States—History—21st century.
Classification: LCC P94.5.A37 B47 | DDC 305.896/073—dc23
LC record available at https://lccn.loc.gov/2019033891
DOI 10.3726/b16689

Bibliographic information published by **Die Deutsche Nationalbibliothek**.
Die Deutsche Nationalbibliothek lists this publication in the "Deutsche
Nationalbibliografie"; detailed bibliographic data are available
on the Internet at http://dnb.d-nb.de/.

The paper in this book meets the guidelines for permanence and durability
of the Committee on Production Guidelines for Book Longevity
of the Council of Library Resources.

© 2020 Venise T. Berry
Peter Lang Publishing, Inc., New York
29 Broadway, 18th floor, New York, NY 10006
www.peterlang.com

All rights reserved.
Reprint or reproduction, even partially, in all forms such as microfilm,
xerography, microfiche, microcard, and offset strictly prohibited.

Printed in the United States of America

Table of Contents

List of Illustrations — vii
Acknowledgments — ix
Introduction: Racialism and the Media — 1

Chapter One: Contemporary Zip Coons: The Problem with Funny — 11
Chapter Two: Ghettofabulous: How Low Can You Go? — 25
Chapter Three: Advertising and Black Folks: Whassup? — 43
Chapter Four: *Black-ish* and the Changing Nature of Black Identity — 55
Chapter Five: Balancing Stereotypes: Black Male and Female Roles on Prime-Time Television — 71
Chapter Six: A Satirical Parody: Black Jesus in the Hood — 85
Chapter Seven: Deconstructing Intersectionality in *Crash* — 99
Chapter Eight: Black Twitter, Interpretive Communities, and Cultural Capital — 109
Chapter Nine: President Barack Obama: Biased Frames and Microaggressions — 127
Chapter Ten: Science Fiction and Fantasy: Going Where Few Blacks Have Gone Before — 139

About the Author — 153

Index — 155

Figures

Figure I.1:   King Kong "Destroy this mad brute" WWII recruitment poster .. 2
Figure 3.1:   Kool-Aid "Old School Flavor" basketball stereotype 45
Figure 3.2:   Dunkin Donuts "Charcoal Donut" ad in Thailand 48
Figure 3.3:   Cheerios "Interracial family" Super Bowl commercial. 49
Figure 3.4:   Gerber "Earn your masters in chewing" placement status 50
Figure 3.5:   Pine Sol "Intensity" reframing the mammy stereotype 51

Acknowledgments

This book is the result of twenty-five years of experiencing, teaching, and researching black images and messages in the media as a black woman in America. I want to thank my students who have been essential to my research and teaching inside and outside of the classroom. I want to thank my family and friends who understand my obsession with the media and love me anyway. They have tolerated and motivated me throughout my career. I want to thank the black actors, writers, directors, producers, and others who have brought to life the stories and characters I love and hate. I want to thank the University of Iowa, the School of Journalism and Mass Communication, and the African American Studies program for continued encouragement and support. Finally, I want to thank my God and savior Jesus Christ who keeps me lifted up.

Introduction: Racialism and the Media

Look at the poster of King Kong. Now imagine replacing King Kong with Los Angeles Lakers's basketball champion Lebron James. Draped across James' left arm is model, Gisele Bundchen in a similar teal dress. His mouth hangs wide open as if he is growling just like King Kong, and in his right hand rather than holding a club he bounces a basketball.

This was the April 2008 cover of *Vogue Magazine*. It perpetuated a number of issues concerning normalized stereotypes, biased racial framing, and problematic historical myths concerning African American culture. For example: the comparison of black men to apes, the notion that black men are obsessed with white women, and the historical myth that black people coming out of Africa are like apes and have an animalistic or violent nature. This cover fueled a significant amount of controversy concerning racists and racism (Hill, 2008; Lebron, 2008; Morris, 2008; Stewart, 2008). The design of the cover is too close to the King Kong poster to argue that it was not the inspiration. So, why would photographer Annie Leibovitz create it? Is she a racist? Why would Lebron James agree to pose like King Kong? Is he okay with racism? Why would *Vogue Magazine* use this image on their cover? Are they comfortable perpetuating racism?

In another example, the recent blockbuster movie *Black Panther* (2018) featured the Jabari Tribe of Wakanda where the leader M'Baku is called Man-Ape. The tribe is known as the White Gorilla Cult and they use the loud, repeated grunt of the gorilla during conflict. The Jabari Tribe also lives in the mountains where it is colder, so they wear fur to cover up. In the movie this tribe displayed an aggressive image that could be connected to the historical myth of black men as apes or black people as animalistic. This was apparently part of the original comic book, written by a white man, but why would a black director and writer Ryan Coogler and Joe Robert Cole keep this stereotypical idea of an ape cult in the movie version? Are they racists? Why would actor Winston Duke play a character where the black man is called a man-ape? Is he okay promoting racism?

The purpose of this book is to explore the notion of racialism. Some people suggest that the first Black American president brought with him a post-racial society. It is obvious that that is not the reality. However, the nature of racial ideology has changed in our society. Yes, there are still ugly racists who push uglier racism, but there are also popular constructions of race routinely woven into mediated images and messages.

Racialism is the normalization of racial images and messages that impact cultural representation. Sometimes it is racist and sometimes it is not. Many media

Figure I.1: King Kong "Destroy this mad brute" WWI Army Recruitment Poster. (Enlist 1917, Library of Congress)

constructions are based on racial images and messages that have become common and accepted in our society today. It is not a good thing, but it also may not be a racist thing.

The *Vogue* cover is similar to the King Kong poster, yet is it possible that photographer Annie Leibovitz is not a racist? With what I know about Lebron James, especially beyond his basketball talent, I don't believe he is okay with racism. And I think *Vogue Magazine* would probably prefer not to perpetuate racism on their cover. I doubt that Ryan Coogler and Joe Robert Cole would be okay with propagating the Jabari tribe as apes if they saw it as a racist image. And I'm sure Winston Duke didn't want to promote racism in the dynamic role he played. So, the question is, how do we explain these racial images and messages outside of the extreme notion of racism? My answer is racialism.

In the twenty-first century, we need a more nuanced understanding of racial constructions. Denouncing anything and everything problematic as racist or racism simply does not work, especially if we want to move toward a real solution to America's race problem. Under the umbrella of racialism, racism is alive and well. Particularly, it encompasses the more historical actions and ideas tied to hate and violence. For example, a white person calling a black person the n-word, hanging a noose in the D. C. National Museum of African American History and Culture, wearing blackface or a KKK robe, and an Alt-Right rally that ends with one person dead and nineteen people injured. These are obvious racist acts. Racism is included under the umbrella of racialism, but my goal is to focus on something else. My focus is on the racial images and messages constructed by the media that do not or should not fall into the loaded category of racism.

Racialism

We live in a society filled with racial situations, messages, practices, and images. In this book, racial constructions are examined using a more nuanced approach. Racialism is a concept that includes, but moves beyond traditional racism. It involves images, ideas, and issues that are produced, distributed, and consumed repetitively and intertextually based on stereotypes, biased framing, and historical myths about African American culture. These representations are normalized through the media, ultimately shaping and influencing societal ideology and behavior.

Specifically, there are four significant areas under the umbrella of racialism. First, the common use of stereotypical images and messages as repetitive ideas about black culture. Second, biased racial framing which involves the shaping and creation of black cultural issues in adverse ways. Third, historical myths such as the derogatory use of knowledge and understanding linked to Africa and African traditions. Fourth, traditional racism involving purposeful hatred and malicious acts.

Sawrikar and Katz (2010) argue against the notion of white supremacy being used synonymously with racism because it situates white as the fixed reference point and places it at a higher social power than all other groups. They discuss the need for cultural competency to become the recognition and acceptance of difference with two components that are key: awareness and sensitivity. This means it is important for a person to make sure they have sufficient knowledge (awareness) about a group and that they challenge (with sensitivity) any stereotypes, biased frames, and historical myths encountered.

Delgado and Stefancic (2012) believe that there is a difference between the ideal notion of racism and the real notion of it. They explain that the ideal focuses on thinking, attitude, and discourse because race is a social construction, not a biological one. They also discuss how racism is used as a means for society to create racial hierarchies allocating privilege and status.

> we may unmake it and deprive it of much of its sting by changing the system of images, words, attitudes, unconscious feelings, scripts and social teachings by which we convey to one another that certain people are less intelligent, reliable, hardworking, virtuous and American than others. (p. 17)

Bonilla-Silva (2014), in his book *Racism without Racists*, suggests that racial discrimination still affects the lives of people of color because new racial constructs are safeguarding the traditional racial order as good as the old ones. He suggests that for most white people, racism is simply an idea or attitude.

> Most contemporary researchers believe that since the 1970's, whites have developed new ways of justifying the racial status quo distinct from the "in your face" prejudice" of the past. Analysts have labeled whites post civil rights racial attitudes as "modern racism," "subtle racism," "averse racism," "social dominance," "competitive racism," or the term I prefer, "colorblind racism". (p. 259)

Carr (1997) believes that the term "racist" itself too often gets confusing.

> The problem is that discrimination is no longer distinguished from its presumed cause, prejudice. Racism became both the cause and effect ... It [the term] does not distinguish between the racism of the oppressor and the oppressed ... There is no way to make this distinction, there is only the term racist, as an ideological phenomenon. (p. 155)

Enlightened racism, as discussed by Jhally and Lewis (1992), moves in this same direction arguing that racial bias is not only about simple skin pigmentation but also cultural class position. Their study of *The Cosby Show* explored how and why white viewers identified with an upper-middle class black family.

> What shows like *The Cosby Show* allow, we discovered, was a new and insidious form of racism. The Huxtables proves that black people can succeed; yet in doing so they also prove the inferiority of black people in general (who have, in comparison to whites, failed). (p. 98)

Racism usually promotes the superiority of white people over black people. And unfortunately, when certain racial issues are normalized within various media products we all buy in. If a child grows up seeing a specific idea or image as ordinary they learn to accept it. For example, when black men are primarily shown as criminals in the news, on prime-time television shows, for popular films, and through gangsta rap music videos, the black man as a criminal becomes the norm. Not only do members of white society start to believe the stereotype but many blacks, even though they know better, start to make assumptions as well.

Doane (2014) says it is problematic to think that diversity works better in a colorblind world or that it is moving us beyond race.

> Diverse casts and commercials, successful athletes and entertainers can all coexist along with racial disparities in income, wealth, poverty, education, and incarceration. The inclusion and upward mobility of 'diverse' individuals do not necessarily challenge the logic and structure of an unequal racial order. (p. 19)

In other words, many scholars are already moving away from the loaded notion of racism, but the necessity for change needs to be explained more clearly. Racialism is a significant product of today's racial ideology. It involves various racial images and messages that are seen everywhere and all the time. Such images and messages are normalized through the media and accepted by society. Too often racialism slips by unnoticed, molded into popular mediated representations.

Critical Race Theory

It is through the lens of Critical Race Theory (CRT) that this book will explore racialism in the media and investigate racialized subjectivities and norms. CRT is effective for exploring the intersection of racialism and the media based on the examination of specific media products and practices. This book is an attempt to identify, critique, and ultimately transform the root causes of racial inequality in selected programs, products, structures and practices of media (Delgado & Sefancic, 2012). Each chapter offers exemplars of racialism operating within mediated experience.

According to Delgado and Stefancic, the structural and systematic influence of certain racial ideology can create oppression, bias, and discrimination. Therefore, it is the goal of CRT to deconstruct those consequences (Rocco, Bernier, & Bowman, 2014). Delgado and Stefancic argue that "racism is an ingrained feature of our landscape, it looks ordinary and natural to persons in the culture" (p. xvi).

Production and programming in the media make up key systems, structures, and practices of knowledge. As the media constructs representations of black culture, it uses racialized words and images. This book presents a cultural critique of how mediated representations and knowledge operates in these production systems using exemplars of racial phenomena, racial effects, and racial hierarchies (Ford & Airhihenbuwa, 2010).

Bell (2000) suggests that racism is a consistency in American society. He says it lies in the center, not the periphery; in the permanent, not the fleeting; in the real lives of black and white people. So, the purpose of my analysis is to think about how we might separate racism (malicious and purposeful hatred) from racialism (consistently normalized mediated racial images and messages). The ultimate goal is to better understand how the media constructs, controls, and manipulates race in our society.

Martinez (2014) suggests that people of color can also be responsible for racism. While some argue that this is rare because racism is tied to power and control, she sees things differently.

> People of color can and do reproduce structures, systems and practices of racism too, but by writing and speaking against the oftentimes one-sided stories existing in a white supremacist world, CRT scholars illuminate the fact that the social world is not static, but is constructed by people with words, stories and also silences. (p. 20)

As more scholars have started to study media and race there is a movement toward the examination of storytelling within CRT. This approach is endorsed by Solorzano and Yosso (2002) who describe how "majoritarian" stories are, "generated from racial privilege and stories in which racial privilege seems natural" (p. 27).

> These stories privilege whites, men, the middle and upper class, and heterosexuals by naming social locations as natural or normative points of reference. A majoritarian story distorts and silences the experiences of people of color and others distanced from the norms such stories reproduce. (p. 23)

Each chapter in this book examines the normalization of racial images and messages in the media, particularly the way they create the basis of our knowledge and understanding when it comes to African American culture in this society and around the world. I see the term racism as having extreme historical and emotional ties pushing it into a deep abyss of negativity, fear, and hatred. When we focus on those extremes, we often miss the important, but subtle elements of racialism that are just as powerful and problematic. For example, the Jezebel stereotype is alive and well in Gabrielle Union's role on *Being Mary Jane*. Despite the fact that she is a highly successful black woman working in the broadcasting industry she jumps in bed with a number of men. And the contemporary mammy stereotype fits Tyler Perry's Madea with her no-nonsense attitude, extreme protective nature, and southern accent thrown in for comedic purposes.

Abraham and Appiah (2006) discuss how the role of visual imagery in the priming of racial stereotypes through the media involves an implicit racial propositioning.

> In this process, the images of blacks function as concrete and vivid cues, exemplars, which provide context that adds to and elaborates understanding of the specific issue discussed explicitly in the text … This process of implicit racial propositioning may be one of the discursive means through which contemporary forms of prejudice manifest themselves, and through which black stereotypes are rehashed and maintained in society. (p. 189)

Despite the fact that we are seeing more African Americans in mediated products today, many of those images and messages reflect certain stereotypes, biased frames, and historical myths. In an effort to open up the conversation about race and media and to promote a move toward change in the status quo, *Racialism and the Media: Black Jesus, Black Twitter and the First Black American President* presents selected exemplars of how race is normalized in the media.

Research has shown that mediated images and messages are an important part of how people see the world (Means-Coleman, 2013; Napoli, 2010; Nightingale, 2011; Ross & Nightingale, 2003). While the media may not have an all-encompassing power or control over an audience, it has been documented that images and messages can impact certain people, at certain times, in certain ways (Newman & Guggenheim, 2011; Potter & Riddle, 2007; Preiss, Gayle, Burrell, Allen, & Bryant, 2007). Mediated texts offer ideas and images that feed our societal norms and ultimately influence how meaning is constructed and deconstructed around the world.

Born out of what sociologist, Herman Gray (1989) calls, "America's storehouse of racial memory," racialism is supported by the historical and ideological distinction between races in this country. As a political construct, it is also tied to social and institutional ideologies and behaviors (Harris-Lacewell, 2003). And finally, the commodification of race through commercialism is another important element to be considered as part of racialism's significant reach (Thornton, 1996).

Chapter One, "Contemporary Zip Coons: The Problem with Funny" examines how the Zip Coon stereotype is alive and well today. It has evolved into a contemporary image in film and television that is very popular. For example, comedians like Eddie Murphy, Kevin Hart, Chris Tucker, and David Mann star in numerous roles as modern day buffoons.

Chapter Two, "Ghettofabulous: How Low Can You Go?" critically explores exemplars in reality TV, rap music, news, film, and urban/street fiction questioning how "ghetto equals black" has become a norm in society.

Chapter Three, "Advertising and Black Folks: Whassup!" focuses on advertising as it uses images of and messages about black culture to sell certain goods and services. This chapter will not only look at negative exemplars, but it will also discuss advertising that frames black culture in a positive way.

Chapter Four, "*Black-ish* and the Changing Nature of Black Identity" offers an exploration of core ideas surrounding blackness. Through this comedy series blackness is challenged and redefined in relation to class, gender, and environment.

Chapter Five, "Balancing Stereotypes: Black Male and Female Roles on Prime-Time Television" explains how complex characteristics can be found in numerous roles on prime-time television that challenge black stereotypes such as Jezebel and Mammy or gang member and criminal.

Chapter Six, "A Satirical Parody: *Black Jesus* in the Hood" investigates how religion and poverty coexist in the inner city. Black Jesus meets the people where they are and in his own way he tries to help everyone understand that life should and could be better.

Chapter Seven, "Deconstructing Intersectionality in *Crash*" is an evaluation of the movie *Crash* which demonstrates how the collision of different genders, classes, and cultures in Los Angeles influences power and experience.

Chapter Eight, "Black Twitter, Interpretive Communities, and Cultural Capital" studies the way that Black Twitter has redefined activism on a global scale by generating a wealth of knowledge and opportunity through shared experience, meaning, and collective behavior.

Chapter Nine, "President Barack Obama: Biased Frames and Microaggressions" evaluates the problematic macro and microaggressions experienced by Obama as the first Black American president. Visual and verbal exemplars are discussed in the perpetuation of biased cultural framing.

Chapter Ten, "Science Fiction and Fantasy: Going Where Few Blacks Have Gone Before" is a critical examination of black themes and characters imagined now and in the future. The world today is fifty percent people of color, so it makes sense that stories about the future in science fiction and fantasy must be more inclusive.

Race will always be a significant part of America's ideological consciousness. As Cornel West (1994) so eloquently wrote, "… a candid examination of race matters takes us to the core of the crisis of American Democracy (p. 156)." Race matters and it will always matter because our societal structure is built on a system of Democracy that depends on it.

The media exemplars studied in each chapter of this book will show that racial phenomena, racial effects, and racial hierarchies are not necessarily the product of racists or racism. Instead racialism, routine images and messages about race have been shaped and sustained through the media over decades then accepted as mainstream ideology and developed into comfortable social behavior.

This book is definitely not an effort to let racists and racism off the hook, but rather a means to expose, deconstruct, and critique other factors that make up racialism. We are technically already there. When scholars use concepts like modern racism, colorblind racism, enlightened racism, averse racism, or subtle racism they are taking a step away. Yet, that one word, racism, still pervades the overall meaning, so I propose this repositioning. We need to think beyond racism in order to better understand the world we live in today. My goal is for *Racialism and the Media* to provoke a serious change when it comes to the problematic racial images and messages that we have all come to know and love.

References

Abraham, L., & Appiah, O. (2006). Framing news stories: The role of visual imagery in priming racial stereotypes. *The Howard Journal of Communications, 17*, 183–203.

Bell, D. (2000). *Race, racism and American law*. New York, NY: Aspen Law and Business Press.

Black Panther. (2018). IMDb. Retrieved from https://www.imdb.com/title/tt1825683/

Bonilla-Silva, B. (2014). *Racism without racists: Color-blind racism and the persistence of racial inequality in America*. Lanham, MA: Rowman and Littlefield.

Carr, L. (1997). *Colorblind racism*. Thousand Oaks, CA: Sage Publishing.

Delgado, R., & Stefancic, J. (2012). *Critical race theory: An introduction* (2nd ed.). New York, NY: New York University Press.

Doane, A. (2014). Shades of colorblindness: Rethinking racial ideology in the United States. In S. Nilsen & S. Turner (Eds.), *The colorblind screen: Television in post-racial America*. New York, NY: New York University Press.

Ford, C., & Airhihenbuwa, C. (2010). Critical race theory, race equity, and public health: Toward antiracism praxis. *American Journal of Public Health, 100*(S1), 30–35.

Gray, H. (1989). Television, black Americans and the American dream. *Critical Studies in Mass Communication, 6,* 376–386.

Harris-Lacewell, M. (2003, November). The heart of the politics of race: Centering black people in the study of white racial attitudes. *Journal of Black Studies, 34*(2), 222–249.

Hill, J. (2008, March 21). LeBron should be more careful with his image. *ESPN.* Retrieved from http://www.espn.com/espn/page2/story?page=hill/080320

Jhally, S., & Lewis, J. (1992). *Enlightened racism: The Cosby Show, audiences, and the myth of the American Dream.* Boulder, CO: Westview Press.

"LeBron James 'Vogue' cover called racially insensitive. (2008, March 24). *USA Today.* Retrieved from https://usatoday30.usatoday.com/life/people/2008-03-24-vogue-controversy_n.htm

Martinez, A. (2014, November). Critical race theory: Its origin, history and importance to the discourses and rhetorics of race. *Frame, Journal of Literary Studies, 27*(2), 9–27.

Means Coleman, R. (2013). *Say it loud! African-American audiences, media, and identity.* New York, NY: Routledge.

Morris, W. (2008, March 31). Monkey business: So is that *Vogue* cover racist or not? *Slate.com.* Retrieved from http://www.slate.com/articles/arts/culturebox/2008/03/monkeybusiness.html

Napoli, P. (2010). *Audience evolution new technologies and the transformation of media audiences.* New York, NY: Columbia University Press.

Newman, W., & Guggenheim, L. (2011). The evolution of media effects theory: A six stage model of cumulative research. *Communication Theory, 21,* 169–196.

Nightingale, V. (2011). *The handbook of media audiences.* Hoboken, NJ: Wiley-Blackwell.

Potter, W., & Riddle K. (2007). A content analysis of media effects literature. *Journalism and Mass Communication Quarterly, 84,* 90–104.

Preiss, R., Gayle, E., Burrell, N., Allen, M., & Bryant, J. (2007). *Mass media effects research: Advances through meta-analysis.* New York, NY: Earlbaum.

Rocco, T., Bernier, J., & Bowman, L. (2014). Critical race theory and HRD: Moving race front and center. *Advances in Developing Human Resources, 16*(4), 457–470.

Ross, K., & Nightingale, V. (2003). *Media and audiences: New perspectives.* New York, NY: McGraw-Hill Education.

Sawrikar, P., & Katz, I. B. (2010). Only white people can be racist: What does power have to do with prejudice? *Cosmopolitan Civil Societies, 2*(1), 80–98.

Solorzano, D., & Yosso, T. J. (2002). Critical race methodology: Counter-storytelling as an analytical framework for education research. *Qualitative Inquiry, 8*(1), 23–44.

Stewart, D. (2008, March 17). Is *Vogue's* Lebron Kong cover offensive? *Jezebel.com.* Retrieved from https://jezebel.com/368655/is-vogues-lebron-kong-cover-offensive

Thornton, S. (1996). *Club cultures: Music, media and subculture capital.* Middletown, CT: Wesleyan University Press.

Vogue Magazine. (2008, April). Lebron James and Giselle Bundchen. Retrieved from https://www.amazon.com/Vogue-April-Issue-Editors-Magazine/dp/B00168A5DM

West, C. (1994). *Race Matters.* New York, NY: Vintage Books.

CHAPTER ONE

Contemporary Zip Coons: The Problem with Funny

Many stereotypes are normalized in our society, especially through the media. Stereotypes are generalizations or overgeneralizations of a group or culture (Brigham, 1971). Unfortunately, many of the normalized stereotypes of African American culture confirm accepted distortions. In his research on implicit stereotypes, Hinton (2017) argues that "culture in mind" is key to influencing the cognition of cultural group members. He believes that stereotypes are predictions and the brain uses predictions based on the structures and meanings experienced in the world (p. 6). Therefore, stereotypes become a resource that enables the transmission of cultural information, specifically within a network where common understandings exist (Kashima & Young, 2010).

Burr (2001) identifies three issues concerning stereotypical images of African Americans in the media.

> First, these images affect how African American children and adults view themselves … Second, these images affect African American adults because others tend to view these images as indicative of how African Americans really act and respond accordingly … Third, these images harm the entire society in that they create disharmony between reality and perception and decrease the chances of positive interactions between blacks and others. (p. 181)

It is important to remember that stereotypes are not inherently racist. Yet, because of their history, many generalizations come from a negative or problematic place. Today, stereotypes are ingrained in our mediated culture as routine. We use them in the everyday process of creating meaning. They are very persuasive and not easy to change.

Social Identity Theory

Social Identity Theory explores group membership and identity arguing that most people identify who they are in society based on the specific groups they belong to, in other words in-group or out-group perspectives (Tajfel & Turner, 1979). Since we exist in a constant cycle of experiencing the world and constructing meaning as members of various groups, Hinton (2000) suggests that we are more likely to accept stereotypes as norms when there is a consensus among friends, family members and even societal groups.

> Social Identity Theory argues that through the cognitive process of categorization and grouping, the in-group members will develop a stereotypical view of the out-group members and through the process of seeking to maintain a relatively high social identity the stereotype of out-group members will tend to be negative. (pp. 114–115)

Hinton also believes that in-group members will view out-group members as more different than they really are from the in-group and they will see out-group members as more similar to each other than they actually are. For example, Banjo (2011) found that white viewers enjoyed stereotypical entertainment based on their cultural openness and competence concerning the out-group.

> Viewers reported low-enjoyment when uncomfortable with entertainment that disparages out-group members and identified conflicts between attitude and behavior when interacting with black culture whether personal or mediated. (p. 153)

Gandy (1998) argues cognitive structural thinking can help us to, "pay attention to the relationships between the attitudes, images, and impressions of self and others as they are shaped through direct and mediated experience" (p. 51). He suggests that priming also helps to normalize racial stereotypes because stereotypes are primed by a certain trait or exemplar which is easily accessible and made applicable to societal perceptions.

Humor and Black Americans

Numerous studies have been conducted to examine how an African American audience relates to humor. Some researchers focus on how humor is used to create joy and understanding, while others examine how it may help to cope with oppression and self-deprecation. For example, black participants reported a more positive attitude and identification when viewing racially charged comedy with black in-group members rather than with white out-group members while white viewers displayed no differences in a 2015 study by Banjo, Appiah, Wang, and others.

Social identity and racial socialization display a direct relationship between the negative stereotypical images received from media, especially when it comes to being black and understanding how blacks identify with their racial group (Adams-Bass, Stevenson, & Kotzin, 2014). Sanders and Ramasubramanian (2012) detailed through their research how most black film and television characters are considered favorable by black audiences despite the fact that many of those images are stereotypical.

A number of studies have explored how to eliminate or counter problematic stereotypes. For example, Holt (2013) found that the fear of crime is becoming more about the human dyad and less about racial stereotypes. Fojioka (1999) studied Japanese students and the negative stereotypes they recognized about African Americans. This research reported that negative stereotypes could be reduced by seeing positive portrayals of African Americans on television.

Tan et al. (2001) studied the social environment and popular roles in order to assess the influence of normative peer groups on changing stereotypes. They reported that peer groups could change the impact of specific stereotypes and they also confirmed that it does not extend to more general racial beliefs. Plus, a combination of critical media consumption and counter message control may reduce some racial stereotypes that are perpetuated by news stories according to a 2007 study by Ramasubramanian. Finally, targeted training against stereotypes can reduce the activation of those stereotypes among audiences based on the research of Kawakami, Dovidio, Hermsen, and others (2000). This means, sometimes people can be motivated to avoid stereotypes when they experience alternative processing.

A few studies have examined the connection between ethnic humor, stereotypes, and media. Reifsteck (2017) discovered that there is a strong correlation between black racial identity and humor specifically when it comes to enjoyment, expression and perception. She reported that exposure to culturally specific humor might also aid in racial identity development. Apte (1987) defined ethnic humor primarily as a type of humor where fun is made of the perceived behavior, customs, personality, or any other traits of a group or its members based on sociocultural identity. Gandy (1998) believes that ethnic humor works because it relies upon readily available stereotypes that make up the core of the joke.

> Telling a joke that depends upon such stereotypes reinforces the symbolic structures in which stereotypes exist and do their cultural work. The joke works because it is understood and we understand or 'get' the joke because we possess knowledge of the stereotype. And, unless our response to the joke is hostile and resistive; getting the joke is likely to increase the structural importance of the stereotype by establishing yet another link for it to the somewhat unique circumstance in the joke. (p. 90)

According to Gillota (2013) there are three broad theories about humor. The first theory, was created by Thomas Hobbes and called "superiority theory." This involves the use of ethnic humor as a way to feel superior to the group that is joked about. The second, is "aggression theory" developed by Sigmund Freud. Aggression theory connects humor to a kind of release valve enabling the discussion of socially unacceptable content. Third, "self-deprecating" humor which is used as a defense among some comedians where they make fun of their own racial group.

Blacks have been the butt of American ethnic humor for a long time argues Cooper (2007). This includes both denigratory and self-denigratory humor. Cooper writes on the comedy of Richard Pryor, "If a humorist makes fun of stereotypes, the implication is that stereotyping is not such a serious issue to the groups so represented (p. 244)." Also, in his study, participants easily recognized Pryor's comedy through the lens of dominant black stereotypes such as cool, tough, ghetto, inferior, poor, lazy, and violent.

According to Bostick (2010), black comedians who speak critically, publicly, and extensively about controversial issues involving the black community claim to be well intentioned, but unfortunately, they may be validating explicit stereotypes. She believes that when stereotypes are validated by these well-known black voices it allows white people (the in-group) to justify those stereotypes about blacks (the out-group).

A Textual/Historical Approach

History can be used to effectively interpret the evolution of a topic or theme. The systematic analysis of stereotypes as they have historically evolved through media programming provides a path toward interpreting primary and secondary texts. Bryant, Black, Land & Porra (2013) believe that history is like a collective memory, "Having a history is important because what happened in the past profoundly affects all aspects of our lives and will affect what happens in the future" (p. 4).

Porra, Hirschelm, and Parks (2014) propose a concept called "cyclical history" which means that the past as reality is unchanging and repeating. They suggest that historical analysis offers a unique potential through scope and duration in which to understand complex phenomena. It is through history that researchers can analyze particular episodes, empirical cases, and patterns of activity according to Smith and Lux (1993).

This chapter analyzes one black stereotype that has evolved throughout history in film and television. It is the examination of specific words, ideas, images, and characteristics that make up particular patterns and themes connected to the Zip Coon stereotype. McKee (2003) argues that this kind of historical analysis can help us understand the way that various cultures and subcultures make sense of who they are.

This analysis examines intertextuality as described by Fairclough (2003), explicitly as it relates to the consistency of the Zip Coon stereotype. It is understood that different cultures may experience different things in different ways, specifically because of intertextuality. And, the interaction of certain images and messages are negotiated within specific historical timeframes.

The Zip Coon Stereotype

The Zip Coon stereotype evolved from minstrel shows in the early nineteenth century (Turner, 1994). Turner explains that the Zip Coon caricature is often presented in colorful, ill-fitting clothing, and he is usually staged as destructive, loud talking, and stupid. According to Jardim (2016), the Zip Coon is an arrogant trickster who avoids responsibility at all costs. Finally, Bogle (1973) described the Zip Coon as a male buffoon who is depicted as an unreliable, subhuman creature misusing the English language for the amusement of white people. Bogle adds that racial stereotypes have been used for decades to confirm white superiority over African Americans.

> All were character types used for the same effect: to entertain by stressing inferiority. Fun was poked at the American Negro by presenting him as either a nitwit or a child-like lackey ... The movies which catered to public tastes, borrowed profusely from all the other popular art forms. When dealing with black characters they simply adapted the old familiar stereotypes, often further distorting them. (p. 4)

In her book *Black Looks: Race and Representation* (1992) bell hooks agrees. She expresses concern because stereotypes are distorted inventions, yet they can be seen as reality.

> Stereotypes however inaccurate are one form of representation. Like fictions they are created to serve as substitutions, standing in for what is real. They are not there to tell it like it is, but to invite and encourage pretense. They are a fantasy, a projection onto the other that makes them less threatening. (p. 170)

The contemporary Zip Coon stereotype has evolved into a prominent media staple. He is the funny, ignorant, aggressive, loud talking, ill-dressed, black male caricature in popular movies and television shows. For example, Stepin Fetchit in *Judge Priest* (1934) and other films during the 1930s took Zip Coon off of the minstrel stage and placed him on the television screen (Fetchit bio). Stepin Fetchit is depicted as a slow-witted, mumbling coon who moves with a lazy shuffle. He scratches his head when he is thinking, uses poor dialogue and his intelligence is questionable.

The Kingfish character was introduced in the *Amos and Andy* radio show (1928–1955) as a Zip Coon stereotype. Freeman Gosden, a white man, did the voice over for radio, but the 1950s television show (1951–1953) used a black actor, Tim Moore (Watkins, 1991). Kingfish displayed the general Zip Coon traits showing a lack of intelligence, plus constantly scheming and trying to con people. For example, he set up a phony raffle, got amnesia whenever it came time to pay his debts, bought and tried to sell a broken-down race horse, and was accused of robbery several times concerning different items.

Despite his standup routines that were often socially conscious and controversial (Trickster, 2010), Redd Foxx in the television sitcom *Sanford and Son* (1972) was a streetwise representation of Zip Coon (Foxx bio). The character of Fred Sanford was a junk dealer living with his only son. He constantly made stupid mistakes, followed get-rich-quick schemes, dished out insults, walked with a stagger and threatened to have a heart attack when confronted about a problem.

Good Times (1972) began as a unique look at life in the urban ghetto, but J.J.'s character eventually developed into an obvious Zip Coon stereotype including his signature action of screaming "dy-no-mite." Jimmy Walker as J.J. also mixed up words showing his illiteracy and flaunted ill-fitting and colorful clothes on his tall, lanky body. Finally, Will Smith in *The Fresh Prince* (1990) brought urban slang and cool pose to upper class Beverly Hills in his more contemporary version of the Zip Coon. His style included wearing a private school jacket inside out to expose the bright red, blue and yellow lining. Since he came from the hood, Will's loud and brash personality was depicted by the upper class kids as cool and different.

The Blaxploitation period meant changes in the Zip Coon stereotype, even though key features continued to thrive under the surface. Confidence in the use of language changed into a jive talk. For example, Rudy Ray Moore used rhyme and signification in his records and movies. "Yes, I'm Dolemite. I'm the one that killed Monday, whooped Tues, put Wednesday in the hospital, called Thursday to tell Friday not to bury Saturday on Sunday" (Dolemite, 1975).

The clothes in many of the Blaxploitation films included bright yellow, red and green suits worn by pimps and players that were promoted as stylish. Black men were depicted as sexually empowered dope dealers and gangsters involved in fighting, shootouts, and other aggressive actions. Bogle (1989) argues that the strained ethnic humor and the inferiority of Black people turned upside-down was used to trick black people into believing that Blaxploitation meant better depictions. But the major characters were superspades with aggressive, take-no-shit attitudes concerning "the man" according to Bogle who argues that the Black Power movement was actually mocked in these films.

Contemporary Zip Coons

Eddie Murphy is definitely a talented actor and comedian, yet his career is built around a number of stereotypes, specifically, the Zip Coon. One of his most controversial characters appeared on *Saturday Night Live* (1998) where he butchered the English language as Buckwheat from the *Little Rascals* (1955). In *the Beverly Hills Cop* series (1984, 1987, 1994), *48 Hours* (1982), *Another 48 Hours* (1990), and *Showtime* (2002) movies his signature laugh, wide-toothy grin and aggressive nature create a comfortable Zip Coon reminder for white and black consumption. And, despite Murphy's enormous skill of being able to portray various members of the Klump family in *The Nutty Professor* (1996), Buddy Love shows up to portray the cool yet ignorant stereotypical Zip Coon.

A number of other popular Murphy characters display Zip Coon characteristics like the jive-talking donkey in the *Shrek* (2001) series, the con artist, street thug Billie Ray Valentine in *Trading Places* (1983) and even the Oscar winning Jimmy from *Dreamgirls* (2006) with his bright suits and third person speech pattern. According to Sands (2018), while not overly racist, a number of Murphy's movies reinforce negative stereotypes. Sands says that throughout Murphy's career, he has been able to appeal to mixed-race audiences by using stereotypes. However, he has also taken the time, occasionally, to celebrate the more positive attributes of blackness in *Coming to America* (1988), *Dr. Dolittle* (1998) and *Daddy Day Care* (2003).

In 2016 Kevin Hart became the highest paid comedian in American history making 87.5 million dollars between June 2015 and June 2016 (Berg, 2016). Hart's movies and television shows like *Jumanji: Welcome to the Jungle* (2017), *Ride Along* (2014), *Ride Along 2* (2016) and *The Real Husbands of Hollywood* (2013) have grossed millions and his stand-up comedy fills huge stadiums like the Staples Center in Los Angeles and Madison Square Garden in New York (Box Office Mojo, 2018).

Many of the characters played by Kevin Hart fall easily into the category of contemporary Zip Coon. For example, *Ride Along* and *Ride Along 2* introduce Ben as a high school security guard who eventually becomes a police cadet. James, played by Ice Cube, is not happy about Ben marrying his sister so he proposes a ride along for Ben. Ben agrees in order to win James's blessing for the wedding while James makes the offer to prove Ben does not deserve his sister. In both movies critics call Ben a clown, a man Smurf and Sir Scream-a-lot. He uses many tired Zip Coon tropes like talking loud, acting stupid, and dressing in bright, colorful, distracting clothes. At different times in the film Hart even imitates an ignorant street hoodlum and an outlandish African Prince.

Get Hard (2015) presents a number of the stereotypical traits related to black men in general and Hart specifically. James, a white, hedge fund manager played by Will Ferrell, is found guilty of embezzlement and sentenced to jail at San Quentin. Although Darnell, Kevin Hart's character, has never been incarcerated he agrees to teach James how to survive in prison. Throughout the film examples of problematic ethnic humor are inserted linking Hart to the Zip Coon including encounters with gangs, prison sex, and urban violence.

A number of roles in Tyler Perry's movies and television shows depict stereotypical characters, but none more obviously than Zip Coon Mr. Leroy Brown played by actor David Mann. In the movie (2008) and television show (2009–2012), both titled *Meet the Browns* this character is as close to the original Zip Coon stereotype as you can get today.

Mr. Brown dresses ridiculously, wearing striped shirts with flowered pants in bright, lively colors like red, blue and yellow. He is portrayed as very stupid with a poor understanding of the English language and he talks constantly about nothing. Mr. Brown's acting efforts are usually over the top including lots of eye popping and hand waving, not to mention his high-pitched whiny voice.

He is the constant butt of the joke. In one television episode, Mr. Brown eats drugged-up brownies and flashes back to the 1970s where he dresses and talks like a stereotypical pimp during the Blaxploitation period. In other episodes, his character continuously offers insults, pranks, and exaggerated movements in response to intense situations. As a matter of fact, in some episodes his degrading ethnic humor gets very extreme. For example, Mr. Brown wets himself, eats rotten food willingly, and even jokes about performing a vasectomy on himself. Svetkey, Watson, and Wheat (2009) express concerned that there is power beyond images in Perry's depictions of black life, so even though Perry believes his characters are simply tools to make people laugh, such comedy mixed with such stereotypes deems black disparity as palatable.

Chris Tucker tends to be a Zip Coon stereotype in most of his movies. In the *Fifth Element* (1997) he is a transgendered Zip Coon, in the *Friday* (1995) movie series he is a pothead Zip Coon and in the *Rush Hour* series (1998, 2001, 2007) he is a crime fighting Zip Coon. Tucker uses all of the conventional Zip Coon elements like bugging his eyes, loud talking, head rolling, misunderstanding and mispronouncing certain words, and displaying an obvious ignorance. Leslie (2001) describes Tucker's character in the *Rush Hour* series a one-dimensional role.

> he's the sidekick, he's the frightened, yet funny dim-witted buddy. It's a role filled with all the standard black stereotypes: he's loud, child-like, dishonest and unable to restrain his emotions when faced with sex and money.

For example, Tucker spends most of his time in *The Fifth Element* screaming in an irritating, high-pitched voice and bugging his eyes. He is dressed in a tight leopard-skin outfit wearing afro puffs or a large white bun. His comedic debut as Smokey in *Friday* focused on how lazy and unreliable his character was. Smokey smoked weed constantly rather than selling it, whipped his neck when he spoke for more emphasis, and jumped around on numerous occasions almost monkey-like.

When Dave Chappelle walked away from a fifty-million dollar contract for his show on *Comedy Central* everyone thought he had lost his mind, but instead he had actually found it. Several years later, Chappelle explained in various interviews that he realized his racial humor was not changing problematic societal perceptions but rather reinforcing them (Cosgrove-Mather, 2006).

Discussing Chappelle's revelation, Bostick (2010) clarified how the context of a joke must be understood in order for someone to actually get it. She says many people do not understand or appreciate black culture enough to make the necessary connections so they laugh at the joke based on face value rather than registering the hypocrisy, sarcasm or satire.

> While jokes about black people by black people may not seem inappropriate; they advance bias depictions of African American traditions, behaviors and cultural norms while offering white people a license to laugh at those stereotypical images. (p. 276)

In their research on *Rush Hour 2,* Park, Gabbadon, and Chernin (2006) found that comedy encourages audiences to naturalize racial differences rather than challenge racial stereotypes. Their findings suggested that many black and white viewers who actively consume comedy derive pleasure from racial jokes.

> Racial stereotypes in comedy are problematic because they help validate racial differences through humor, thus rendering them natural and unchallengeable. Because racial stereotypes in comedy rarely offend the audiences and are presented in an enjoyable way, audiences are able to naturalize specific knowledge about racial minorities without resistance. (p. 173)

So, it is possible that the white crew member who made Dave Chappelle uncomfortable when he laughed at the sketch about "Black Pixies" (Farley, 2005) was not necessarily a racist, but he simply enjoyed a certain comfort level because of the way stereotypes have been naturalized in our society. It is possible with racial images and messages consistently perpetuated by the media and accepted in society a person does not have to be a racist to laugh at racial ideas or create racial content.

Hinton (2000) maintains that stereotypes reflect faulty thinking about a group or culture, and some people may not be aware because of the prominence and consistency of the humorously focused images and messages. This means that the active monitoring of our own cognitive process is necessary to create oppositional or counter-stereotypical strategies for the elimination of such stereotypes (Fiske, 1984).

As Entman (1992) discussed in his article on news, modern racism and cultural change it is easy for people to fall into stereotypical thinking, especially when normalized stereotypes are promoted consistently and intertextually.

> Because old-fashioned racist images are socially undesirable, stereotypes are now more subtle and stereotyped thinking is reinforced at levels likely to remain below conscious awareness. Rather than the grossly demeaning distortions of yesterday, stereotyping of blacks now allows abstraction from and denial of the racial component. (p. 345)

Humor, fuels conversations, challenges assumptions, and stretches social boundaries often with stereotypical images and messages just under the surface. According to Amditis (2013), the continued use of racial stereotypes in humor today contributes to the preservation of the current racial hierarchy making the fight for a better racial climate more difficult.

> The difficulty involved in identifying, processing, interpreting, comprehending, and retaining the subtle and symbolic undertones when exposed to humor is the key to understanding the ultimate harm that is done by the use of stereotypical tropes and tactics in comedy. (p. 5)

Humor is usually based on stereotypical ideas and images. Stereotypes through humor provide easily recognized and understood historical impressions of how members of black culture might think and act. Unfortunately, when ethnic humor is based on normalized and accepted stereotypes racialism is involved and that means there is a problem with funny.

References

48 Hours. (1982). IMDb. Retrieved from http://www.imdb.com/title/tt0083511/
Adams-Bass, V., Stevensen, H., & Korzin, D. (2014). Measuring the meaning of black media stereotypes and their relationship to the racial identity, black history knowledge, and racial socialization of African American youth. *Journal of Black Studies, 45*(5), 367–395.
Amditis, J. (2013, May). White men can't joke: Racial hierarchy and traditional race narratives in humor and comedy. Retrieved from http:/www.academia.edu/3539690/White_Men_Cant_Joke_Racial_Hierarchy_And_Traditional_Race_Narratives_in_Humor_and_Comedy [Accessed 1 Apr].
Amos and Andy [TV Show]. (1951–1953). IMDb. Retrieved from http://www.imdb.com/title/tt0043175/
Amos and Andy [Radio Show]. (1928–1955). Retrieved from https://www.amosandandy.org/
Another 48 Hours. (1990). IMDb. Retrieved from http://www.imdb.com/title/tt0099044/
Apte, M. (1987). Ethnic humor vs. 'sense of humor': An American sociocultural dilemma. *American Behavioral Scientist, 30*, 27–41.
Banjo, O. (2011). What are you laughing at?: Examining white identity and enjoyment of black entertainment. *Journal of Broadcast and Electronic Media, 55*(2), 137–159.
Banjo, O., Appiah, O., Wang, Z., Brown, C., & Walther, W. (2015). Co-viewing effects of ethnic oriented programming: An examination of in-group bias and racial comedy exposure. *Journal of Mass Communication Quarterly, 92*(3), 666–680.
Berg, M. (2016, September 27). The highest paid comedians 2016: Kevin Hart dethrones Jerry Seinfeld as cash king of comedy with $87.5 million payday. *Forbes Magazine*. Retrieved from https://www.forbes.com/sites/maddieberg/2016/09/27/the-highest-paid-comedians-2016-kevin-hart-out-jokes-jerry-seinfeld-with-87-5-million-payday/#453270e7320e
Beverly Hills Cop series. (1984, 1987, 1994). *IMDb*. Retrieved from https://www.imdb.com/title/tt0092644/
Bogle, D. (1973/1989/1994/2001). *Toms, coons, mulattoes, mammies and bucks: An interpretive history of blacks in films*. New York, NY: Continuum & Bloomsbury.
Bostick, C. (2010). A barrel of laughs or a river of tears: The problem with African Americans using comedy to air dirty laundry in critical race perspectives. *Georgetown Journal of Law and Modern Critical Race Perspectives, 2*(2), 257–276.
Box Office Mojo. (2018, February 12). Kevin Hart. Retrieved from http://www.boxofficemojo.com/people/chart/?id=kevinhart.htm

Brigham, J. C. (1971). Ethnic Stereotypes. *Psychological Bulletin, 76,* 15–38.
Bryant, A., Black, A., Land, F., & Porra, J. (2013). What is history? What is IS history? And why even bother with history? *Journal of Information Technology, 28*(1), 1–17.
Burr, S. (2001). Television and societal effects: An analysis of media images of African Americans in historical context. *Gender, Race and Justice, 4*(J), 159–181.
Cooper, E. (2007). Is it something he said: The mass consumption of Richard Pryor's culturally intimate humor. *The Communication Review, 10,* 233–247.
Cosgrove-Mather, B. (2006, February 3). Dave Chappelle: 'I wasn't crazy'. *CBS/AP.* Retrieved from https://www.cbsnews.com/news/dave-chappelle-i-wasnt-crazy/
Dixon, T. (2008). Network news and racial beliefs: Exploring the connection between national television news exposure and stereotypical perceptions of African Americans. *Journal of Communication, 58,* 321–337.
Dreamgirls. (2006). IMDb. Retrieved from http//www.imdb.com/title/tt0443489/
Entman, R. (1992, Summer). Blacks in the news: Modern racism and cultural change. *Journalism Quarterly, 69*(2), 341=361.
Fairclough, N. (2003). *Analyzing discourse: Textual analysis for social research.* New York, NY: Routledge.
Farley, C. J. (2005, May 14). Dave speaks. *Time.* Retrieved from http://content.time.com/time/magazine/article/0,9171,1061512-6,00.html
Fetchit, Stepin [Biography]. IMDb. Retrieved from http://www.imdb.com/name/nm0275297/bio
The Fifth Element. (1997). IMDb. Retrieved from http//www.imdb.com/title/tt0119116/
Fiske, J. (1984). *Social cognition.* Reading, MA: Addison-Wesley.
Fojioka, Y. (1999, Spring). Television portrayals and African American stereotypes: Examination of television effects when direct contact is lacking. *Journalism and Mass Communication Quarterly, 76*(1), 52–75.
Foxx, Redd [Biography]. Retrieved from https://www.biography.com/people/redd-foxx-9300106
The Fresh Prince. (1990–1996). IMDb. Retrieved from http://www.imdb.com/title/tt0098800/
Friday. (1995). IMDb. Retrieved from http://www.imdb.com/title/tt0113118/
Gandy, O. (1998). *Communication and race: A structural perspective.* New York, NY: Oxford University Press.
Get Hard. (2015). IMDb. Retrieved from http://www.imdb.com/title/tt2561572/
Gillota, D. (2013). *Ethnic humor in multiethnic America.* New Brunswick, NJ: Rutgers.
Good Times. (1974–1979). IMDb. Retrieved from http://www.imdb.com/title/tt0070991/
Hinton, P. (2000). *Stereotypes, cognition and culture.* Philadelphia, PA: Taylor and Francis.
Hinton, P. (2017). Implicit stereotypes and the predictive brain: Cognition and culture in "biased" person reception. *Palgrave Communication, 3,* 17086, 1–9. Retrieved from https://doi.org/10.1057/palcomms.2017.86
Holt, L. (2013, January 10). Writing the wrong: Can counter-stereotypes offset negative media messages about African Americans. *Journal of Mass Communication Quarterly, 90*(1), 108–125.

hooks, b. (1992). *Black looks: Race and representation.* Boston, MA: South End Press.
Jardim, S. (2016, July 26). Recognizing racist stereotypes in U.S. media. *Medium.com.* Retrieved from https://medium.com/@suzanejardim/reconhecendo-esteriótipos-racistas-internacionais-b00f80861fc9
Judge Priest. (1934). IMDb. Retrieved from http://www.imdb.com/title/tt0025335/
Jumanji: Welcome to the Jungle. (2017). Retrieved from http://www.imdb.com/title/tt2283362/
Kashima, Y., & Young, V. W. L. (2010). Serial reproduction: An experimental simulation of cultural dynamics. *Acta Psycholigica Sinica, 42*(1), 56–71.
Kawakami, K., Dovidio, J., & Hermsen, M. (2000, May). Just say no (to stereotyping): Effect of training on the negation of stereotypical associations on stereotype activation. *Journal of Personality and Social Psychology, 78,* 871–888.
Leslie, M. (2001, September). Coon show, kung fu and Chris Tucker. *Michigan Citizen.* Retrieved from http://proxy.lib.uiowa.edu/login?url=https://search-proquest-com.proxy.lib.uiowa.edu/docview/368103569?accountid=14663
The Little Rascals. (1955). IMDb. Retrieved from http//www.imdb.com/title/tt0278213/
McKee, A. (2003). *Textual analysis: A beginners guide.* London, England: Sage.
Meet the Browns. (2008). IMDb. Retrieved from http//www.imdb.com/title/tt1047494/
Meet the Browns [TV Series]. (2009–2012). IMDb. Retrieved from http://www.imdb.com/title/tt1319598/
Moore, R. R. (Actor). (1975). *Dolemite.* IMDb. Retrieved from http://www.imdb.com/name/nm0601834/
The Nutty Professor. (1996). IMDb. Retrieved from http://www.imdb.com/title/tt0117218/
Park, J., H., Gabbadon, N., & Chernin, A. (2006). Naturalizing racial differences through comedy: Asian, black and white views on racial stereotypes in *Rush Hour 2. Journal of Communication, 56,* 157–177.
Porra, J., Hirschheim, R., & Parks, M. (2014, September). The historical research method and information systems research. *Journal of the Association for Information Systems, 15*(9), 536–576.
Ramasubramanian, S. (2007, Summer). Media based strategies to reduce racial stereotypes. *Journalism and Mass Communication Quarterly, 84,* 249–264.
The Real Husbands of Hollywood. (2013). IMDb. Retrieved from http://www.imdb.com/title/tt2608368/
Reifsteck, T. (2017). The relationship of black racial identity and aggressive humor. *Modern Psychological Studies, 22*(2), 37–49.
Ride Along. (2014). IMDb. Retrieved from http://www.imdb.com/title/tt1408253/
Ride Along 2. (2016). IMDb. Retrieved from http//www.imdb.com/title/tt2869728/
Rush Hour. (1998). IMDb. Retrieved from https://www.imdb.com/title/tt0120812/
Rush Hour 2. (2001). IMDb. Retrieved from https://www.imdb.com/title/tt0266915/
Rush Hour 3. (2007). IMDb. Retrieved from https://www.imdb.com/title/tt0293564/
Sanders, M., & Ramasubramanian, S. (2012). An examination of African Americans' stereotyped perceptions of fictional media characters. *Howard Journal of Communications, 23*(1), 17–39.

Sands, Z. (2018). *Film comedy and the American dream.* New York, NY: Taylor and Francis.

Sanford and Son. (1972–1977). IMDb. Retrieved from http://www.imdb.com/title/tt0068128/

Saturday Night Live. (1998). Eddie Murphy as Buckwheat. Retrieved from http://www.imdb.com/title/tt0274795/

Showtime. (2002). IMDb. Retrieved from http://www.imdb.com/title/tt0284490/

Shrek. (2001). IMDb. Retrieved from http://www.imdb.com/title/tt0126029/

Smith, R., & Lux, D. (1993). Historic method in consumer research: Developing causal explanations of change. *Journal of Consumer Research, 19*(4), 595–610.

Svetkey, B., Watson, M., & Wheat, A. (2009, March 20). How do you solve a problem like Madea? *Entertainment Weekly.* Retrieved from http://eds.a.ebscohost.com.proxy.lib.uiowa.edu/ehost/detail/detail?vid=0&sid=35916b79-15b3-4761-b9b185d31eef21c5%40sessionmgr4008&bdata=#AN=37005658&db=f5h

Tajfel, H., & Turner, J. C. (1979). An integrative theory of intergroup conflict. In W. G. Austin & S. Worchel (Eds.), *The Social Psychology of Intergroup Relations.* Monterey, CA: Brooks/Cole.

Tan, A., Tan, G., Audeyena, T., Crandall, H., Fukushi, Y., Nyandwi, A., ... Wu, C. (2001, July–September). Changing negative stereotypes: The influence of normative peer information. *Howard Journal of Communication, 12,* 171–180.

Trading Places. (1983). IMDb. Retrieved from http://www.imdb.com/title/tt0086465/

A Trickster and a Foxx Website. (2010). Retrieved from https://ignitiontoremix.wordpress.com/more-best-of/a-trickster-and-a-foxx/

Turner, P. (1994). *Ceramic uncles and celluloid mammies: Black images and their influence on culture.* New York, NY: Anchor Books.

Watkins, M. (1991). What was it about 'Amos and Andy'? *The New York Times.* Retrieved from https://www.nytimes.com/1991/07/07/books/what-was-it-about-amos-n-andy.html

CHAPTER TWO

Ghettofabulous: How Low Can You Go?

Not all African Americans live in poverty or in the inner city, yet somehow American society seems to believe that black equals ghetto. In her book *Ghetto Nation*, Cora Daniels (2007) argues that in the twenty first century ghetto no longer refers to where you live but how you live.

> It is a mindset, and not limited to a class or a race. Some things are worth repeating: ghetto is not limited to a class or a race. Ghetto is found in the heart of the nation's inner cities as well as the heart of the nation's most cherished suburbs; among those too young to understand (we hope) and those old enough to know better; in little white houses, and all the way to the White House; in corporate corridors, Ivy League havens, and, of course, Hollywood. (p. 8)

Ghettofabulous is a problematic pop culture frame that refers predominantly to a bias about black culture displaying extreme tendencies like loud talking, garish dressing, bling blinging, fighting, and certain levels of ignorance. It has become a repetitive image in pop culture where white college students throw ghettofabulous parties (Wise, 2010), Miley Cyrus's twerks at a VMA performance (Hare, 2013), Cardi B holds a $500K ghettofabulous baby shower (Heller, 2018), average women flaunt long nails with extreme manicures like Niecy Nash in *Claws* (Penrice, 2018), and a California yoga studio gives out do-rags for their booty-shaking, ghettofabulous classes (Baker, 2013).

Domonoske (2014) said, in a *NPR* interview, the word "ghetto" has evolved from meaning a segregated, restricted neighborhood to an individual context such as acting, dressing or talking.

> [It is] Being ghetto, or behaving in a low-class manner (see also ratchet). Ghettofabulous, flashy glamour without the wealth. Ghetto as an adjective, roughly synonymous with jury-rigged, for anything cobbled together out of subpar materials.

Daniels (2007) adds that ghetto as a state of mind is hard to describe but easy to recognize. For example, she spots an ice cream truck rolling down the streets of Brooklyn blasting Lil John's "Okaaaaay," she watches a contest on *VH1* where they are searching for Nelly's Miss Apple Bottom (a regular girl with an irregular waist to butt ratio), she lambasts the Oscar nominated film *Hustle and Flow* when the pimp-wanna-be-rapper sings "Beat that Bitch," she complains about young people who are calling each other baby daddies or baby mammas (a term she sees as dismissive), she admits frustration concerning the number of youth living in today's depressing culture of nihilism and self-destruction, and she wonders why in school if a black child is not ghetto then they are seen as "acting white." Because the popularity of ghetto in American society is based on a lack of self-respect, Daniels worries most of all that too many of these biased frames embrace the worst instead of the best of black culture.

Giles (2010) defines media framing as the process by which a topic is presented from a particular angle (or a variety of angles), inviting audiences to draw particular conclusions, and to make particular allusions to other topics. Entman (2007) describes the process of biased framing as introducing or raising the salience and importance of certain ideas, to some extent getting audiences to think, feel or decide in a particular way.

> The text contains frames, which are manifested by the presence or absence of certain key words, stock phrases, stereotypical images, sources of information, and sentences that provide thematically reinforcing clusters of facts or judgements. (p. 52)

In this chapter, the biased framing of black culture as ghettofabulous on television, in film, through rap music, for news, and as urban fiction is explored. According to Mukherjee (2006), ghettofabulous offers new standards of cool and the spectacle within popular media emerges less as subcultural resistance and more as hegemonic cooptation through capitalism.

Ghettofabulous in Television

Reality television shows like *The Real Housewives of Atlanta* (2008) and *Love and Hip Hop* (2010) are the ideal exemplars for ghettofabulous TV. Audiences tune in each week to watch African American women and men cussing, arguing, fighting, and displaying certain levels of ignorance. To some extent that problematic and biased frame has become a staple when it comes to rap music and hip hop, but *The Real Housewives of Atlanta* (*RHOA*) features a number of prominent black women who became stars in their own right, yet still fit the mold. For example, Kandi Burris-Tucker is a Grammy award winning singer, songwriter, and entrepreneur formerly part of the popular group Xscape (Mitchell, 2017). Cynthia Bailey is a supermodel who has walked the runways of New York, Paris, and Mulan. She owns the Bailey Agency School of Fashion in Atlanta (Anderson, 2013). Kenya Moore was named Miss USA in 1993 and landed in the top six for the Miss Universe pageant (Hensley, 2016). Eva Marcille won the third season of Americas Next Top Model and has since become an actress, television host, and entrepreneur (Koerner, 2017).

Of course, there are other cast members who have built their fame and fortune from the show. For example, NeNe Leakes' has milked ghettofabulous for all it is worth. Her original claim to fame before *RHOA* was as a stripper, but she has now launched a one-woman comedy show, appeared on *Glee* as a swim coach, co-hosted the *Today Show*, and acted on Broadway in *Cinderella* (Ferrise, 2018). Portia Williams went from a subservient athlete's wife to a co-host on the nationally syndicated talk show *Dish Nation* (Ho, 2014).

The display of ghettofabulous in *RHOA* is obvious. There are ostentatious pictures of expensive houses, cars, and name brand products in every episode (Hawley, 2014). Each cast member seems eager to outshine the other when it comes to conspicuous consumption. On Season 4, NeNe Leakes told Sheree Whitfield (former cast member) "I am very rich, Bitch!" (Orr, 2019). Orr discusses how over several seasons, Whitfield and Kenya Moore battled about the size and quality of their homes: "Chateau Sheree" vs. "Moore Manor."

Baby showers and weddings are ghettofabulous. Kenya Moore created a fairytale shower filled with princess ballgowns, tiaras, gold wigs, crowns, and capes in a room staged like a royal court, including an enchanted forest, with an oversized gold throne (Quinn, 2018). When Kandi Burress married Todd Tucker they had a *Coming to America* themed wedding that included African Dancers, drummers, and real lions (Palacios, 2015). Finally, Phaedra Parks ordered 12 different birthday cakes for her son's first birthday party (Parks, 2012).

The cat fights among these upper-class, grown women are constant and ugly. For example, Sheree Whitfield got into a lot of battles. She and Marlo Hampton went at it in Africa when Marlo was purposely excluded from an activity (Lucas, 2012), she pulled off the wig of former *RHOA* cast member Kim Zolciak, and had an argument with her party planner Antony that resulted in the popular phrase "Who gonna check me, boo?" (Moylan, 2014). Kandi Burress has gone several rounds with various cast members as well including Portia Williams who she attacked for accusing Burress of planning to drug her for sex (Mathers, 2018). Burress and Phaedra Parks fell out behind a business deal with Burress's husband, and later Burress was livid when she found out that the drugging allegation originally came from Parks (Quinn, 2017).

Sexuality and looks are over-the-top on the show. Kandi Burrus has launched a line of sex toys as part of her internet show *Kandi Coated Nights* (2018–) and produced a sold-out burlesque show in Atlanta. During Episode 12 in Season 11, the housewives visit Japan and in one crude scene they pretend that a pickle is a dick and imitate various sexual acts on each other. There are stories about some of the women having breast implants, liposuction, nose jobs, and butt lifts. The clothes that many of the cast members wear usually expose large sections of their huge breasts, thick thighs and wide bottoms. Parks and Moore even had a ridiculous blow up in Season 5 concerning the production of a DVD video that ended in a controversy over "stallion booties" vs. "donkey booties" (IMDb, 2013).

Empire (2015–) has been ranked as the number one broadcast drama among the 18 to 49 demographic (Berg, 2017). There have been many situation comedies, but a prominent black drama is rare on prime-time television. It is not surprising this black drama on television about a successful music company is ghettofabulous. The show is riddled with controversy based on the stereotypes perpetuating ghetto life including criminals, murderers, drug dealers, and thugs. The executive-producer, director Lee Daniels says, "It's all set against a "boughetto" (that's bougie + ghetto- try to keep up) backdrop of gunplay, glitz and gold diggers" (Williams, 2015).

Cookie Lyons played by Taraji Henson is a ghettofabulous character described by her stylist as flaunting a classy-hood style (Hope, 2015). When she is released from prison Cookie is wearing big hoop earrings, a white fur jacket, and a tight-fitting leopard print dress from the 1980s (Jones, 2015). Unfortunately, her wardrobe doesn't change much once she is back in the real world.

> In one instance she might wear an Alexander McQueen dress with a Balenciaga clutch. In another moment she might wear a rhinestone tiger-striped dress with a long slit up the side. She uses a big Chanel gold pendant, Cavalli necklaces, and Gucci python bags to accessorize her leopard jumpsuits. (Wright, 2018, pp. 93–94)

Wright adds that Cookie's character is constantly slipping between hustler and music mogul. Dr. Boyce Watkins called the show "Ghettofied Coonery" on

CNN in a discussion with Don Lemon (Emery & Bennett, 2015). Watkins said, "A lot of black actors and actresses are tired of being put in the entertainment ghetto. The entertainment ghetto is basically the place where you have roles … specifically designed for black people, where black actors are kind of locked into" (Emery & Bennett, 2015).

Niecy Nash has solidified her spot in *Claws*, a ghettofabulous dramedy on *TNT*. Nash plays Desna, the owner of a nail salon who launders money for the mafia, commits and covers up murders, but takes care of her crew who are known for their unique, over-the-top manicures. Nash wears signature tight fitting, low-cut jumpsuits, emphasizing her big breasts, small waist, and large behind (Carter, 2017). Her character also enjoys hood-style bling with rings on every finger, big silver chain belts, gold bangles, huge dangling earrings and necklaces, and, of course, long dazzling fingernails (Cutler, 2017). In a 2018 NPR interview, Nash said at five-years-old she told her grandmother that she wanted to be, "Black, fabulous and on TV" (Sanders & Sastry, 2018). She has definitely accomplished that.

Ghettofabulous in Urban Fiction

Waiting to Exhale by Terry McMillan was released in 1992 and it became a huge success. The book sold four million copies, it was followed by a sequel and became a hit movie. Because of the success of *Waiting to Exhale* the doors to publishing opened wide for African American women's fiction. Fast forward twenty years later, African American Women's fiction has, for the most part, been replaced at large publishing companies by urban/street fiction which is flying off the shelves.

This new focus on negative black stereotypes of male thugs and female hoochies has made urban/street fiction the perfect genre to push into the mainstream. James Fugate the owner of *Eso Wan Books* in Los Angeles expressed his concerned, "The ghetto lit being written today is mostly 'mindless garbage about murder, killing, thuggery. When you read this ghetto lit nothing happens to your mind. And that is the problem" (Daniels, 2007, p. 65).

Research in this area suggests that remedial learners are more engaged with urban fiction. Specifically, the stereotypes, sexual themes, and violence serves to lure them in despite poor reading achievement (DeBlaze, 2003; Mahiri, 2004; Morris, Hughes-Hassell, Agosto, & Cottman, 2006; Rampey, Dion, & Donahue, 2009; Stovall, 2005; Townsend, Thomas, Neilands, & Jackson, 2010). Gibson (2016) produced a study on African American girls reading urban fiction and found that outside of class urban fiction was very popular. She suggested that street lit could be used as a bridge to interest African American girls in other reading genres.

In 2005, Stovall reported that a variety of readers from a broad range of class backgrounds were reading urban fiction. This report worried Pollard (2015) who argued that the depiction of drug culture, poverty, criminal violence, and hypersexuality in the genre was creating an unrealistic trope of authenticity fueled by market driven expectations. However, a student experiment, by Bean and Moni (2003) used urban fiction to motivate critical discourse concerning racial images and messages. They offered the storylines as a way to challenge negative representations and cultural stereotypes, along with questioning beliefs about identity. Gibson (2016) taking that same approach discovered that African American girls were able to demonstrate some of the critical literacy skills necessary to challenge such stereotypes and problematic representations in urban/street fiction.

When problematic images and messages are promoted and accepted through the publishing industry, researchers, librarians, and teachers racialism is at work. There is no denying that *The Coldest Winter Ever* (1999) by Sista Souljah was the catalyst for popularizing urban fiction. And the problem, as Fugate expressed earlier, was that the main character, Winter, had absolutely no growth in the story. She was stupid at the beginning of the book and stupid at the end.

Book stores today are filled with ghettofabulous stories about black inner-city life that promotes ignorance and glorifies violence. Some of the obvious titles include: *Thugs and the Women Who Love Them* (Clark, 2002), *Crackhead and Crackhead II* (Lennox, 2012a, b), *Murderville* (Coleman, 2012), *Gangsta* (K'wan, 2014), *The Dopeman's Wife* (Coleman, 2014), and *Nasty Girls* (Gray, 2007).

Munshi (2015) wrote about an urban fiction couple Ashley and Jarvis Coleman. Not only do they write urban/street fiction, but they met in a ghettofabulous way. According to the article in *Financial Times*, Jarvis was sixteen-years-old, running from the police when he threw nine ounces of cocaine into 15-year-old Ashley's back yard. Ashley stashed the drugs for him and they have been together ever since. The couple started out reading urban fiction books together, then one day they decided to write one, Today, they each write approximately 5,000 words daily finishing a book in approximately three weeks. This is one of the many criticisms concerning urban/street fiction, the lack of quality. A book written in three weeks usually reads like it was written in three weeks.

Ghettofabulous in News

The unique difference when it comes to thinking about ghettofabulous in the news is that the news is real. In his song "Ghetto Fabulous," Dr. Dre says no matter how much money you make you have to stay true to the game. Halnon (2011) argues that the way to stay true is to situate oneself in materialistic culture while at the same time maintaining authenticity which means keeping a connection to the street.

> On the consumer side this means that media representations of the black ghetto require certain realities to support the popular image such as real thugs, real gangs, real gangbanging, real drug dealing, and the real selling of women ... the authentic value of black ghetto cool is contingent upon the harsh material realities of everyday African American inner-city life. (p. 4)

The crossover between pop culture images of the ghetto and the real inner city are very important. Loury (1998) wrote that the legacy of slavery lingers in our cities' ghettos. He believes there is problem with the color line when it comes to the lower class.

> These black ghetto dwellers are a people apart, susceptible to stereotyping, stigmatized for their cultural styles, isolated socially, experiencing an internalized sense of helplessness and despair, with limited access to communal networks of mutual assistance. Their purported criminality, sexual profligacy, and intellectual inadequacy are the frequent objects of public derision. In a word, they suffer a pariah status. It should not require enormous powers of perception to see how this degradation relates to the shameful history of black-white race relations in this country. (Loury, 1998)

We see this pariah status in the news often. For example, one news headline reads, "In Chicago, One Weekend, 66 shooting victims and Zero Arrests" (Oppel & Harmon, 2018). The article reports that the shootings were concentrated on the west and south sides of the city which are areas known for high crime and high levels of gang activity. Another headline, "Baltimore is the Nation's Most Dangerous City" was in *USA Today*. It cites city officials as saying that gangs and drug activity are responsible for the high crime numbers (Madhani, 2018). A third headline from *FiveThirtyEight* speaks for itself, "Black Americans are Killed at 12 Times the Rate of People in Other Developed Countries" (Silver, 2015).

In his memoir, rapper and actor Ice T said crime is about making easy money, "There is something sexy about crime because it takes a lot of courage to fuck the system."

> On mass media screens today, whether television or movies, mainstream work is usually portrayed as irrelevant, money is god, and the outlaw guy who breaks the rules prevails. Contrary to the notion that black males are lured by the streets, mass media in patriarchal culture has already prepared them to seek themselves in the streets, to find their manhood in the streets, by the time they are six years old. (hooks, 2004, p. 27)

Dixon's research (2008) suggests that exposure to the network news often confirms black stereotypes such as blacks are poor and intimidating. Oliver's study (2003) suggests that the power of black male stereotypes is real and examined how black men are often misidentified and assumed guilty based on bias frames. When crime victims were white, eye witnesses often described black suspects in stereotypical terms according to a study from the University of British Columbia. In that study, Jacobs (2016) found that white victims and black perpetrators tended to be seen through a stereotypical lens, specifically when it came to the more violent crimes.

Images in the news also send certain messages concerning black culture generally. Wing (2017) argues that the mainstream media sometimes treats white killers better than black victims. He reviewed a plethora of news stories that demonstrated how officials seemed dismissive or unsympathetic to black victims some even blaming them for their own deaths. Wing's research showed that stories about black victims become character assassinations, while white criminals are written from a more positive and empathetic perspective. The article, included examples for black victims like, "Montgomery's latest Victim had a history of narcotics abuse, tangles with the law" (*Ala.com*, 2014), "Travon Martin was suspended from school three times" (*NBC News*, 2013), and "Police: Warren shooting victim was a gang member" (*WKBN*, 2014). Along with examples for white criminals, "Santa Barbara Shooting: Suspect was soft spoken, polite, a gentleman, ex-principal says" (*Whittier Daily News*, 2014), "Oregon School Shooting Suspect fascinated with guns but was a devoted Morman, his friends say" (*FOX News*, 2014), and "Ala. Suspect brilliant, but social misfit" (*Lubbock-Avalanche Journal*, 2010).

An extensive study on news and opinion media conducted by Dixon (2017) found that many outlets misrepresent blacks in association with criminality, poverty, welfare recipients, and generally instability. His two-year study reviewed more than 800 news stories reported distorted representations, inaccurate information, and racially biased coverage which is a serious problem. Finally, Jan (2017) explains that media outlets routinely show poor black families as dependent and disfunctional while white families are usually depicted as stable. She cites a 2017 report by racial justice organization Color of Change that suggests political rhetoric and public policy are often fueled by stereotypes like absentee fathers, criminality and poverty in the inner city.

Ghettofabulous in Rap Music

In real life, according to a report by Lewis (2015), rapper Brandon Duncan known as Tiny Doo was charged with nine counts of gang conspiracy and faces 25 years in prison. Although Duncan did not shoot anyone, he was apparently linked to the gang responsible for a number of shootings when his mixed tape was released a year later.

Because a couple of his songs described the murders in detail the prosecutor added Duncan to the court order. This means, if the gang is convicted, the prosecutor plans to argue that Duncan promoted and benefitted from their illegal acts (Lewis, 2015).

Just like Duncan, other rappers have found it difficult to break the link between real crime and rap music. As a matter of fact, in order to maintain their authenticity as mentioned earlier many believe that they need to stay connected to the streets. A timeline constructed by Emmett (2018) shows a series of clashes that rapper, actor T.I. has had with the law. In May of 2018, T.I. was arrested for disorderly conduct and public drunkenness. In 2010, he went to prison for eleven months for drug charges and parole violations. In 2009, he struck a plea deal and was sentenced to a year and a day for weapons possession as a convicted felon. In 2001, 2002, and 2004 he was arrested for illegal gun possession. In 1998, T.I. served a year in prison for the manufacturing and distribution of cocaine.

Gangsta rap exploded into the mainstream in the late 1980s. In the beginning, traditional record companies had a hard time with this music labelling it as not really music. So, rap music during the early period had to embrace the inner-city streets for funding and support. Drug dealers became record moguls with companies called Death Row, Ruthless Records, and Bad Boy Records. In the mid 1990s rap music was bought up by mainstream music corporations.

According to Quinn (2004), in these corporations gangsta rap involved a number of major themes: social cultural commentary, authenticity, nihilism, and commercialism. This music placed the anger and frustration of young black men up front with controversial songs like "F--- the Police" by NWA, "Cop Killer" by Ice T and "Geto" by the Geto Boys. Rap music encompassed other problematic frames as well when it came to black culture such as misogency, sexism, hypermasculinity, drug use, homophobia, and greed. For example songs like Snoop Dogg's "Doggystyle," "The Chronic" by Dr. Dre, "Bling Bling" by Gucci Mane, and "Rich Niggaz" by Juvenile popularize negative images and messages.

As Donalson (2007) explains, "by the 1990's a number of popular rappers and Hip Hop producers had taken their market appeal into that celebrated American area labeled 'entrepreneurship ... where their celebrity status and financial success is staggering" (p. 131).

Rap music and Hip Hop made the ghetto cool, crime and all. The negativity of inner-city life was absolved in a blast of money, sex, and power. Younge (2005) in *The Guardian* talks about how the beats and rhymes of rap music easily tapped into free market capitalism.

> There's fabulous. And then there's ghetto-fabulous ... Fabulous is meant to be desirable—classic, pricey, and proper. Ghetto-fabulous is meant to be deplorable—crude, crass, vulgar, and vile. Fabulous is for the urbane, who buy gold by the ounce and call

it jewelry; ghetto-fabulous is for the urban, who by their gold by the pound and call it bling. (p. 1)

Rapper Lil Jon is the self-proclaimed King of crunk. Apparently crunk is the feeling of being crazy drunk (Daniels, 2007). Lil Jon is the perfect example of ghettofabulous as he raps through a gold grill, wearing huge gold chains, and dark glasses. Many of his videos promote misogyny and women in tight clothes twerking, or fighting in water. He has suggestive song titles like "Get Low," "Act a Fool," "Madness," and "I don't Give a F---" feeding into the genre's ignorance.

Despite the power that she has built in the rap industry, Nicki Minaj produces videos and lyrics that can be labeled ghettofabulous as well. The sexual nature of her words and movements leave very little to the imagination. In a song called "Good Form" (2018) with Lil Wayne she falls right into the misogynistic trash heap as her dancers perform an erotic dance and she raps, "I let him eat the cookie cause it's good for him and when he eat the cookie he got good form." Soon, Lil Wayne drops in a few lines talking about "women as bitches with asses jumpin' [gotta] get on his dick turn it into a pipe bomb." There was a recent controversy concerning Minaj's wax figure at Madame Tussauds in Berlin where she is not standing but positioned on her knees and dressed provocatively in ghetto fashion (Matthews, 2020).

Finally, in a song titled "Act Ghetto" (2015) by Tyga featuring Lil Wayne the lyrics say all that needs to be said.

> She just wanna act ghetto. She just wanna dance like a stripper, rap like a nigga. She just wanna rub her titties, pop her ass. She just wanna act ghetto when the cameras flash ... She wear diamonds on her pussy, diamonds on her neck. Talking out her neck, demanding respect. Yeah, she wanna act ghetto getting drunk on the set. Gonna drink it out the bottle, flip the finger when she ready ... (Tyga).

> ... Ghetto fabulous, she so booty-ful. She ain't got home training, she got Uber tho. She just texted me O-M-W with two XO's. Only thing she always coming through is project hoes. Gotta put my jewelry up, gotta hide the dough ... (Lil Wayne)

Ghettofabulous in Film

Poverty and violence seem to encompass the image of inner-city ghettos in most films. A plethora of films perpetuated the inner city during the late 1990s reflecting ghettos as gang and drug infested hell holes. This includes, *New Jack City*, *Boyz N the Hood*, *Juice*, *Menace II Society*, *Colors*, *Clockers*, *Gang Related* and others. There was one movie in this group that offered a more balanced look at the ghetto environment, *Boyz N the Hood* (1991).

The recent 25 year anniversary of *Boyz N the Hood* has enabled scholars to rethink the impact of this film. Written and directed by the later John Singleton, *Boyz* was one of the first in this genre to offer a more contextual look at what was happening in the inner-city. Tre and Ricky live in the hood, Crenshaw South Central Los Angeles, but they are not involved with gangs and drug dealers. Ricky's older brother DoughBoy is a gang member and he has also served time in jail. Ricky and Doughboy are being raised by a single mother, while Tre's mother decides he should live with his father, Furious, because he started getting into trouble at school.

The film shows the good and bad of black communities. For example, there are good and bad characters like Furious who works and owns his home and Tre who receives important lessons from his father about responsibility, economic stability and respecting women. Ricky and Doughboy's mother Brenda is usually shown at home in a house robe, so it doesn't look like she has a job. She makes a difference between her two sons based on their projected futures. Ricky has the possibility of going to college on a football scholarship while Doughboy is connected to gangs and jail.

Black cops can be as bad as white cops in the film. When someone breaks into Furious's house, the police take a long time to show up and when they do arrive the black police officer insults Furious. Tre and Ricky are targeted by a gang and Ricky is ultimately killed. Doughboy and his crew seek revenge. Tre joins them at first, but soon realizes he is in over his head and drops out. At the end of the movie, Tre graduates and goes off to Moorhouse College while Doughboy is killed.

Singleton's main message in *Boyz* was that boys need fathers to help them grow into men. That message was challenged by Jones (1991) who felt like it suggested that single women could not raise strong, positive men. Walcott (1992) agreed, voicing concern that Singleton's stance was dismissive of the countless single mothers who have raised successful black sons inside and outside of the hood.

The movie often referred to women as bitches and hoes, but there are a few scenes that were different. For example, when one girl at a barbeque asks Doughboy why he always calls girls those names he replies, "Cause that's what you are." On the other hand, at a picnic when the food is ready Tre tells the guys that they need to let the women get in line first to show respect. Tre's girlfriend Brandi lives on the block. She has both a mother and father at home and attends a catholic school. Brandi is waiting for marriage to have sex, but she is there for Tre when he needs her.

Baps (1997) by Robert Townsend is a film all about ghettofabulous. *BAPS* stands for Black American Princesses. In the movie two ghettofabulous homegirls move to Los Angeles to live their dream as video dancers. Because Nisi looks like a younger version of a dying millionaire's maid, the nephew comes up with a scheme to have Nisi pretend to be the granddaughter of the maid to secure an inheritance. The *BAPS* dress in loud colors, wear tight clothing, butcher the English language. Nisi wears an extreme blonde hairdo with a gold tooth and a leopard-skin jumpsuit.

Bogle (2001) says this kind of visual distortion has been directed at black women's images since film became a popular form of mass media. He complains that old familiar stereotypes are adopted and distorted when diverse cultural experiences of black women are needed instead. Mukherjee (2006) studies the *Barber Shop* series as a case study concerning cultural productions of the ghetto fabulous aesthetic and she finds similar problems.

> the audacious poses of bling serve, more than markers of class emulation, as embodied substantiation of the fabulousness of the ghetto, emphatic affirmations of working class, urban black life. Answering capitalism with uber-capitalistic success, bling performs specifically racial work, positing blackness as social asset and the ghetto as reservoir of rebellious creativity and stylish daring. (p. 600)

Mukherjee argues that these films are tales of working-class black life in the urban ghetto that celebrate black business spaces through sites of refuge and renewal. In her analysis of *Barber Shop*, she moves ghettofabulous away from the traditional bling seen as irresponsible and into a more complex examination of class transcendence through business. For example, Calvin is all about the bling when we first meet him in the film admiring an eight-bedroom guesthouse owned by Oprah. But as the story unfolds Calvin starts to understand the problem with unchecked commercialism and focuses on the importance of a strong black work ethic instead.

Ghetto equals place, ghetto equals lifestyle, ghetto equals cool, and ghetto equals fabulous. Halnon (2011) writes that the ghetto has not only been racialized in this society, but commodified as black authenticity.

> The ghetto and ghettoized as products have become so many occasions for selling fads, fashions, and media. It is what sells coveted authenticity in a society of the spectacle where the market obliterates authenticity. Black ghetto cool exemplifies the vicious circle: the derivation of authenticity because of the market and the selling back of it through the market as ghetto cool. (p. 3)

Black conspicuous consumption is part of the American dream which includes key elements of bling such as luxury cars, designer labels, and expensive jewelry. To be ghettofabulous is to maintain an "I'm getting paid" attitude related to class according to a *New York Times* article by Givhan (2000). Mukherjee (2006) focuses on the audacious spectacle of conspicuous commodity consumption too.

> the ghettofabulous aesthetic has left its mark on a range of cultural productions from music videos to ghetto lit, fashion to film, walking a familiar line from defiance to bowdlerization, from raucous wild child of the streets to co-opted product tagline. (p. 1)

Finally, Wright (2018) sees ghettofabulous as more than an economic issue. "A person's race, gender, wealth, and location are part of the definition of social class" (p. 100). And, Johnson (2003) warns that black authenticity is a trope too often manipulated for cultural profit. He sees blackness as an appropriated commodity, a complex and nuanced racial signifier contingent on historical, social, and political production. So, as the biased framing of a ghettofabulous black culture is tied directly to various mediated products American society rests in the comfort of normalizing and accepting those images and ideas. What must be taken into account is that through the practice of appropriation ghettofabulous leaves the black community and consumes society as a whole.

References

Anderson, J. C. (2013, April 18). Cynthia Bailey's side hustle success secrets: How one real housewife is leveraging her 15 minutes. *Huffpost*. Retrieved from https://www.huffingtonpost.com/2013/04/17/cynthia-bailey-side-hustle-secrets_n_3104248.html

Baker, K. (2013, September 4). Santa Barbara yoga studio gives out do-rags at ghetto fabulous class. *Jezebel*. Retrieved from https://jezebel.com/santa-barbara-yoga-studio-gives-out-do-rags-at-ghetto-1251090792

BAPS. (1997). IMDb. Retrieved from https://www.imdb.com/title/tt0118663/

Bean, T & Moni, K. (2003, May). Developing students' critical literacy: Exploring identity construction in young adult fiction. *Journal of Adolescent and Adult Literacy, 46*(8), 638–648.

Berg, M. (2017, March 20). How *Empire* became the most valuable show on broadcast television. *Forbes*. Retrieved from https://www.forbes.com/sites/maddieberg/2017/03/20/how-empire-became-the-most-valuable-show-on-broadcast-tv/#7e3296a85063

Bogle, D. (2001). *Toms, coons, mulattoes, mammies and bucks: An interpretive history of blacks in American films*. New York, NY: Continuum International Publishing.

Boyz N the Hood. (1991). IMDb. Retrieved from https://www.imdb.com/title/tt0101507/

Carter, K. (2017, June 8). Niecy Nash's *Claws* is the future of television. *The Undefeated*. Retrieved from https://theundefeated.com/features/niecy-nash-claws-tnt/

Clark, W. (2002). *Thugs and the women who love them*. New York, NY: Dafina Books.

Coleman, J. (2014). The Dopeman's Wife. New York: Urban Books.

Coleman, A. & Coleman, J. (2012). *Murderville*. New Orleans: Cash Money Content.

Coming to America. (1988). IMDb. Retrieved from https://www.imdb.com/title/tt0094898/

Cutler, J. (2017, January 15). TNT's summer drama "Claws" nails women's friendships. *Media Village*. Retrieved from https://www.mediavillage.com/article/tnts-summer-drama-claws-nails-womens-friendships/

Daddy Day Care. (2003). IMDb. Retrieved fromhttps://www.imdb.com/title/tt0317303/

Daniels, C. (2007). *Ghetto Nation: A journey into the land of bling and the home of the shameless*. New York: NY: Doubleday.

Deblaze, G. (2003). Acknowledging agency while accommodating romance: Girls negotiating meaning in literacy transitions. *Journal of Adolescent and Adult Literacy, 46*(8), 642–635.

Dish Nation. (2011–). IMDb. Retrieved from https://www.imdb.com/title/tt1973047/

Dixon, T. (2008). Network news and racial beliefs: Exploring the connection between national Television news exposure and stereotypical perceptions. *Journal of Communication, 58*, 321–337.

Dixon, T. (2017, December). A dangerous distortion of our families. *Color of Change Report*. Retrieved from https://s3.amazonaws.com/coc-dangerousdisruption/full-report.pdf

Donalson, M. (2007). *Hip Hop in American cinema*. New York, NY: Peter Lang.

Domonoske, C. (2014, April 27). Segregated from its history: How 'ghetto' lost its meaning. *Code Switch NPR*. Retrieved from https://www.npr.org/sections/codeswitch/2014/04/27/306829915/ segregated-from-its-history-how-ghetto-lost-its-meaning

Dr. Dolittle. (1998). IMDb. Retrieved fromhttps://www.imdb.com/title/tt0118998/

Emery, D., & Bennett, A. (2015, March 18). *Empire* under fire: Black scholar on *CNN* calls show 'ghettofied' 'coonery.' *The Wrap*. Retrieved from https://www.thewrap.com/empire-under-fire-black-scholar-calls-show-ghettofied-coonery/

Emmett, N. (2018, May 16). TIMELINE: Rapper T.I.'s arrests, legal trouble throughout the years. *AJC*. Retrieved from https://www.ajc.com/news/local/timeline-rapper-arrests-legal-trouble-throughout-the-years/tn1qJ4VlKyF2XpBbtrH79J/

Empire. (2015–). IMDb. Retrieved from https://www.imdb.com/title/tt3228904/

Entman, R. (2007). Framing bias: Media in the distribution of power. *Journal of Communication, 57*, 163–173.

Ferrise, J. (2018, May 3). *Real Housewives* star NeNe Leakes on why you should be a gold digger. *InStyle*. Retrieved from https://www.instyle.com/news/real-housewives-nene-leakes-gold-digger-money

Fujioka, Y. (2005). Black media images as a perceived threat to African American ethnic identity: Coping responses, perceived public perception, and attitudes towards affirmative action. *Journal of Broadcasting & Electronic Media, 49*, 450–467.

Gandy, O. H. (2001). Racial identity, media use, and the social construction of risk among African Americans. *Journal of Black Studies, 31*(5), 600–618.

Gibson, S. (2016). Adolescent African American girls as engaged readers: Challenging stereotypical images of black womanhood through urban fiction. *Journal of Negro Education, 85*(3), 212–224.

Giles, D. (2010). *Psychology of the media*. London, England: Red Globe Press.

Givhan, R. (1999, October 9). Rapper attitude in designer diamonds and furs: Ghetto fabulous goes global. *The New York Times*. Retrieved from https://www.nytimes.com/1999/10/09/news/rapper-attitude-in-designer-diamonds-and-furs-ghetto-fabulous-goes.html and https://psmag.com/news/racial-stereotypes-shape-eyewitnesses-memories

Givhan, R. (2000, October 14). Ghetto fabulous glitter fades. *The New York Times*. Retrieved from https://www.nytimes.com/2000/10/14/news/ghetto-fabulous-glitter-fades.html

Gray, E. (2007). *Nasty girls*. New York, NY: St, Martins Press.

Hare, B. (2013, August 26). Miley Cyrus twerks, stuns VMA Crowd. *CNN Entertainment*. Retrieved from https://www.cnn.com/2013/08/26/showbiz/music/miley-cyrus-mtv-vmas-gaga/index.html

Halnon, K. (2011, May). So called black ghetto cool: From the colorline to the colorblind. *Consumers, Commodities and Consumption, 12*(2). Retrieved from https://csrn.camden.rutgers.edu/newsletters/12-2/halnon.htm

Hawley, A. C. (2014, Spring). An image rarely seen: *The Real Housewives of Atlanta* and the televisual image of the African American woman. Iowa Research online. Dissertation. Retrieved from https://ir.uiowa.edu/cgi/viewcontent.cgi?referer=https://www.google.com/&httpsredir=1&article=5155&context=etd

Heller, C. (2018, June 21). Cardi B wants a "lit" baby shower. *ENews* https://www.eonline.com/news/945967/cardi-b-wants-her-baby-shower-to-be-lit

Hensley, C. (2016, June 8). Miss USA just crowned its ninth black woman—now meet the first eight. *The Tempest*. Retrieved from https://thetempest.co/2016/06/08/social-justice/race/miss-usa-crowned-its-ninth-black-woman-so-who-were-the-first-eight/

Ho, R. (2014, August 6). Porsha Williams named permanent host on *Dish Nation*. *AJC*. Retrieved from https://www.ajc.com/blog/radiotvtalk/exclusive-porsha-williams-named-permanent-host-dish-nation/LlkYpQevlKSzvMEo0VkP1N/

hooks, b. (2004). *We real cool: Back men and masculinity*. New York, NY: Routledge.

Hope, C. (2015, January 28). *Empire* stylist explains Cookie's bossed-up fashion game. *Jezebel*. Retrieved from https://themuse.jezebel.com/empires-stylist-explains-cookies-bossed-up-fashion-game-1682261202

Jacobs, T. (2016, May 13). Racial stereotypes shape eyewitness memories. *Pacific Standard*. Retrieved from https://psmag.com/news/racial-stereotypes-shape-eyewitness-memories

Jan, T. (2017, December 13). News media offers consistently warped portrayals of black families, study finds. *The Washington Post*. Retrieved from https://www.washingtonpost.com/news/wonk/wp/2017/12/13/news-media-offers-consistently-warped-portrayals-of-black-families-study-finds/?noredirect=on&utm_term=.82d4664bc50c

Johnson, E. P. (2003). *Appropriating blackness: Performance and politics of authenticity*. Durham, NC: Duke University Press.

Jones, J. (1991). The new ghetto aesthetic. *Wide Angle, 13*(3–4), 40–51.

Jones, T. (2015, January 26). How *Empire's* top stylist makes cast look like a million bucks. *New York Post*. Retrieved from https://nypost.com/2015/01/26/empire-stylist-reveals-fashion-secrets-of-hit-tv-show/

Kandi Coated Nights. (2018–). IMDb. Retrieved from https://www.imdb.com/title/tt8543080/

Koerner, A. (2017, November 2). *Real Housewives of Atlanta* star Eva Marcille isn't the same women who won *America's Next Top Model* 13 years ago. *Bustle*. Retrieved from https://www.bustle.com/ p/real-housewives-of-atlanta-star-eva-marcille-isnt-the-same-woman-who-won-americas-next-top-model-13-years-ago-3193050

K'wan. (2014). *Gangsta*. Wyandanch, NY: Urban Books.

Lennox, L. (2012a). *Crackhead*. Columbus, OH: Triple Crown Publications.

Lennox, L. (2012b). *Crackhead II*. New York, NY: Atria Books.

Lewis, K. (2015, March 7). When rap music is a crime. *The Atlantic*. Retrieved from https://www.theatlantic.com/politics/archive/2015/03/when-rap-music-is-a-crime/386938/

Loury, G. (1998, March 1). An American tragedy: The legacy of slavery lingers in our cities' ghettos. *Brookings*. Retrieved from https://www.brookings.edu/articles/an-american-tragedy-the-legacy- of-slavery-lingers-in-our-cities-ghettos/

Love and Hip Hop [TV Series]. (2010). IMDb. Retrieved from https://www.imdb.com/title/tt1718437/

Lucas, D. (2012, February 1). Real talk: *The Real Housewives of Atlanta* cat fight. *Essence.com*. Retrieved from https://www.essence.com/news/real-talk-lessons-from-the-rhoa-fight/

Madhani, A. (2018, October 1). Baltimore is the nation's most dangerous big city. *USA Today*. Retrieved from https://www.usatoday.com/story/news/2018/02/19/homicides-toll-big-u-s-cities-2017/302763002/

Mahiri, J. (2004). New literacies in a new century. In *What they don't learn in school: Literacy in the lives of urban youth* (pp. 1–18). New York, NY: Peter Lang.

Make an Ass out of a Donkey. (2013). IMDb. Retrieved from https://www.imdb.com/title/tt2632272/

Mathers, R. (2018, March 31). Kandi VS. Porsha, NeNe VS. Kim, and Kenya VS. Marlo in new RHOA reunion trailer. *Celebrity Insider*. Retrieved from http://celebrityinsider.org/ kandi-vs-porsha-nene-vs-kim-and-kenya-vs-marlo-in-new-rhoa-reunion-trailer-watch-tyrone-gilliams-call-nene-leakes-a-stalker-130894/

Matthews, D. (2020, January 7). New Nicki Minaj was statue at Madame Tussauds in Berlin baffles fans. *New York Daily News*. Retrieved fromhttps://imgbin.com/png/pUtDqtGB/compton-prayer-black-jesus-png

McMillan, T. (1992). *Waiting to Exhale*. New York, NY: Penguin Random House.

Minaj, N. & Lil Wayne. (2018). *Good Form*. Retrieved from https://www.google.com/search?ei=R0mgXPWiCe2MtgX6kIvICQ&q=good+form+by+minaj&oq=good+-form+by+minaj&gs_l=psyab.3..0i22i30l8.11930.11930..13416...0.0..0.90.90.1......0....1..gws-wiz.JocoR0tJZmU

Mitchell, J. (2017, February 7). Get paid to be yourself: The business of being Kandi Burruss. *Forbes*. Retrieved from https://www.forbes.com/sites/julianmitchell/2017/02/07/get-paid-to-be-yourself-the-business-of-being-kandi-burruss/#7fb959ec1ce2Forbes

Mitchell, A. (2017, September 29). *America's Next Top Model* winner Eva Marcille joins *The Real Housewives of Atlanta* part-time. *Celebrity Insider*. Retrieved from http://celebrityinsider.org/americas-next-top-model-winner-eva-marcille-joins-real-housewives-of-atlanta-part-time-71820/

Morris, V., Hughes-Hassell, S., Agosta, D., and Cottman, D. (2006). Street lit flying off teen fiction bookshelves in Philadelphia Public Libraries. *Young Adult Library Services*, 5(1), 16–23.

Moylan, B. (2014, March 19). The 20 best *Real Housewives* fights. *Vulture*. Retrieved from https://www.vulture.com/2014/03/best-real-housewives-franchise-fights.html

Mukherjee, R. (2006). The ghetto fabulous aesthetic in contemporary black culture. *Cultural Studies*, 20(6), 599–629.

Munshi, N. (2015, November 13). Urban fiction: Words on the street. *Financial Times*. Retrieved from https://www.ft.com/content/08785ece-86ee-11e5-9f8c-a8d619fa707c

Oliver, M. B. (2003, September). African American men as "criminal and dangerous": Implications of media portrayals of crime on the criminalization of African American men. *Journal of African American Studies*, 7(2), 3018.

Oppel, R., & Harmon, A. (2018, August 6). In Chicago, one weekend, 66 shooting victims and zero arrests. *The New York Times*. Retrieved from https://www.nytimes.com/2018/08/06/us/chicago-weekend-shootings.html

Orr, N. (2019, January 29). *The Real Housewives of Atlanta* show how impossible the American dream is. *BuzzFeed News*. Retrieved from https://www.buzzfeednews.com/article/nielaorr/real-housewives-of-atlanta-nene-leakes-kenya-moore-debt

Palacios, N. (2015, June 4). *Real Housewives of Atlanta's* Kandi Burrus' movie inspired wedding. *Inside Weddings*. Retrieved from https://www.insideweddings.com/weddings/kandi-burruss-and-todd-tucker/560/

Parks, P. (2012, March 21). A piece of cake. *Bravo TV*. Retrieved from https://www.bravotv.com/the-real-housewives-of-atlanta/season-4/blogs/phaedra-parks/a-piece-of-cake

Penrice, R. R. (2018, August 8). Meet Morgan Dixon, the Black Girl Magic behind the incredible nail art on TNT's hit series *Claws*. *The Root*. Retrieved from https://theglowup.theroot.com/meet-morgan-dixon-the-black-girl-magic-behind-the-incr-1828082044

Pollard, C. (2015). The p-word exchange: Representing black female sexuality in contemporary urban fiction. In Trimico Melancon (Ed.), *Black Female Sexualities*, New Jersey: Rutgers University Press.

Rampey, B., Dion, G., & Donahue, P. (2009). *The nations report card: Trends in academic progress in reading and mathematics* (2008). Retrieved from: nces.ed.gov/nationsreportcard/pubsmain2008/2009479.asp

Quinn, D. (2017, May 14). Phaedra Parks admits to mistakes she made with Kandi Burruss: I was being petty. *People*. Retrieved from https://people.com/tv/phaedra-parks-admits-to-mistakes-she-made-with-kandi-burruss-rhoa-recap/

Quinn, D. (2018, October 21). Kenya Moore celebrates baby-to-be with majestic fairytale-themed baby shower. *People Magazine.* Retrieved from https://people.com/ parents/kenya-moore-baby-shower-rhoa/

Quinn, E. (2004). *Nuthin' but a g thang: The culture and commerce of gangsta rap.* New York, NY: Columbia University Press.

The Real Housewives of Atlanta. (2008–). *Bravo TV.* Retrieved from https://www.bravotv.com/the-real-housewives-of-atlanta

Sanders, S & Sastry, A. (2018, June 19). Neicy Nash, living a dream: To be black, fabulous and on TV. *NPR.* Retrieved from https://www.npr.org/2018/06/14/620120303/niecy-nash-on-claws

Silver, N. (2015, June 18). Black Americans are killed at 12 times the rate of people in other developed countries. *FiveThirtyEight.* Retrieved from https://fivethirtyeight.com/features/black-americans-are-killed-at-12-times-the-rate-of-people-in-other-developed-countries/

Souljah, S. (1999). *The Coldest Winter Ever.* New York, NY: Simon and Schuster.

Stovall, T. (2005). Parental guidance: Gangsta lit do you really know what your teenagers are reading? *Black Issues Book Review, 7*(4), 56–57.

Townsend, T., Thomas, A., Neilands, T., & Jackson T. (2010). I'm no Jezebell: I am young, gifted and black: Identity, sexuality and black girls. *Psychology of Women Quarterly, 34,* 273–285.

Tyga, featuring Lil Wayne. (2015). "Act Ghetto". *A-ZLyrics* Retrieved from https://www.azlyrics.com/lyrics/tyga/actghetto.html

Waiting to Exhale. (1995). IMDb. Retrieved from https://www.imdb.com/title/tt0114885/

Walcott, R. (1992). Keeping the black phallus erect: Gender and the construction of black masculinity in *Boyz N the Hood. Cineaction, 30,* 68–74.

Williams, S. (2015, March 11). The cookie conundrum: Is *Empire* wrong to portray black as criminals? *The Daily Beast.* Retrieved from https://www.thedailybeast.com/the-cookie-conundrum-is-empire-wrong-to-portray-blacks-as-criminals

Wing, N. (2017, September 21). When the media treat white suspects and killers better than black victims. *HuffingtonPost.* Retrieved from https://www.huffingtonpost.com/entry/when-the-media-treats-white-suspects-and-killers-better-than-black victims_us_59c14adbe4b0f22c4a8cf212

Wise, T. (2010, February 26). Majoring in minstrelsy: White students, blackface and the failure of mainstream multiculturalism. *Racism Review.* Retrieved from http://www.racismreview.com/blog/2010/02/26/majoring-in-minstrelsy-white-students-blackface-and-the-failure-of-mainstream-multiculturalism/

Wright, J. (2018). *Empire and black images in popular culture.* Jefferson, NC: McFarland.

Younge, G. (2005, October 16). Urbane, not urban: how wealthy whites do ghetto-fabulous too. *The Guardian.* Retrieved from https://www.theguardian.com/world/2005/oct/17/usa.comment

CHAPTER THREE

Advertising and Black Folks: Whassup!

Introduction

Advertising is an area where racialism is very prominent. I have collected many examples over the years of problematic images and messages surrounding African American culture. Meaning is constructed in advertising using various levels of knowledge concerning black culture. Those constructions sometimes include racist images along with stereotypes, biased framing, and historical myths.

Barthes (1972) believes that levels of interpretation can present different meanings for different people. For example, the concept of polysemy is often used to explain how the same sign or text can produce a variety of interpretations among the same audience (Edwards, Edwards, Wahl, & Meyers, 2016). According to Barthes, "levels of meaning can be found in tri-dimensional links that are part of a semiological chain of communication. The first link of the chain is the sign or denotative idea involving a literal or common meaning directly from the text. The second link is the signifier or connotative idea where an additional layer of meaning brings enhanced dimension to the communication process. The third link involves myth and with this new layer of meaning there is a deeper understanding usually tied to historical and/or ideological knowledge" (p. 113).

In 1990, Dates and Barlow identified what they considered a major problem with racial stereotypes and media in their book *Split Images* and that problem still exists today.

> Black media stereotypes are not the natural, much less harmless, products of an idealized popular culture; rather they are more commonly socially constructed images that are selective, partial, one-dimensional, and distorted in their portrayal of African Americans. (p. 5)

Advertisements can be read as cultural texts. Crocker (2009) believes that culture is one of the most powerful influences in society today, and much of the time that power is not noticed. He adds that some companies wrap their product in bold aspects of culture while others use more subtle elements. A more nuanced example is Nike's embrace of Colin Kaepernick after the controversy over his kneeling during the National Anthem in order to bring awareness to the issue of Black Lives Matter. The Nike ad featured Kaepernick's face with the slogan, "Believe in something, even if it means sacrificing everything" (Burns, 2018). An obvious example would be the use of Chance the Rapper singing "break me off a piece of that Kit Kat bar (Gibbs, 2016).

Chambers (2008) describes the evolution of blacks in the advertising industry, specifically the efforts of black professionals to alter the stereotypical perceptions of African Americans. He explains how the depictions of everyday life in advertising influence consumer's perceptions of who they are.

> In presenting that vision, however, advertising personnel made no effort to be inclusive or even accurate. Instead, they addressed their work to the most powerful group: those consumers who had the economic power to buy and thus uphold the market society (p.4).

It was when black people became part of the market society that images and messages started to change. When advertisements reproduce stereotypes, racial bias, historical myths and even racism they participate in the process of reinforcing negative societal ideology.

Racialism Exemplars in Advertising

Let's take a look at the Kool-Aid ad in Figure 3.1 below. A young black couple sits on the front steps of an apartment building enjoying a glass of Kool-Aid. The text at the bottom reads "old school flavor" which is depicted by the style of dress including the boy's classic Kangol hat, hush puppies and afro, as well as the large

Figure 3.1: Kool-Aid "Old School Flavor" Basketball stereotype

framed glasses both are wearing. Two issues arise in the study of this ad. First, there is the stereotype that black people love red Kool-Aid, but that one is okay because the purpose of the ad is to sell Kool-Aid. However, the second issue involves the basketball under the boy's foot.

This notion is tied to another common stereotype about black men. There is no reason for a basketball to be in this photo. He is obviously not on a basketball court or even wearing tennis shoes, so the basketball in this ad links to the stereotype of African American males as athletes.

In two interesting ads collected over the years, the United Colors of Benetton and Pizza Hut offer very different views of race relations. The Benetton ad showed two girls hugging, but only the white girl is smiling. Her golden hair is lit as if to signify a halo or an angel while the black girl's hair is shaped into two horns tying her to the image of a devil (Benetton Group, 1991). On the other hand, the Pizza Hut ad sent a positive message about race relations because both girls were smiling and hugging cheek to cheek. The tag line read "Pizza is a lot like life".

The makers of Barbie in an effort to be more inclusive have apparently run into several controversies. In one instance, a black Barbie was designed unlike the white Barbies with cleavage and wearing a low-cut top to emphasize her chest (Fontaine,

2009). Then recently another black Barbie lit a fuse when she was designed with one side of her hair in dark brown cornrows and on the other side a long blonde weave (Yang, 2018).

The wording in an ad can also be problematic. For example, a promotion for the *Smothers Brothers Comedy Hour* was created as reruns were about to be aired on *E Television* a few years ago. The ad presented a photo of President Kennedy and a photo of Malcolm X. Under the photo of President Kennedy it read, "Some people were born great." Under the photo of Malcolm X it read, "Some people achieved greatness." This is an example of how wording matters because it is possible that Malcolm X was born great too, but he was not born rich.

Another even more powerful example of how racial wording can be misused occurred during Hurricane Katrina when two photos were circulated with similar images described very differently based on race. In one photo a white male and female are wading through water carrying bags. The caption read, "Two residents wade through chest deep water after finding bread and water from a local grocery store …" The second photo showed a young black male wading through water carrying a large bag and the caption read, "A young man walks through chest deep water after looting a grocery store …" (Jones, 2017).

An ad from *NBC* proudly proclaims "More colorful" with twenty or more of their hosts featured. The term colorful must have referred to the feathers on the abstract peacock that serves as their logo, because not one face on that ad belonged to a person of color (Schneider, 2009). And finally, Epson computers who now uses Shaq as a spokesperson once took out a three-page ad where on the first page they declared "Our lasers are aimed at everyone." Then on the next two pages it is revealed that everyone included only an Asian man, a white woman, and two white men.

One of the worst examples I've found was a promotion in *TV Guide* for a telelvision show called *Class of 1996*. The show, about a group of college students who become friends, didn't stay on the air long because it was marketed so poorly. The full page ad was riddled with problems of racialism. In the top left corner was a small photo of a white male and female laughing, next to that was another photo with three white students also happy. In the middle of the page sitting all by himself and looking very sad was the young black male college student. Another photo filled the lower third of the page. It was supposed to show the entire group of friends, except the black character was missing. My question—why is the black male left out of the bottom photo? But then after looking more closely he was not gone completely because his arms were actually laying on the left side of the table. In other words, his body had literally been cut out of the photo, but his arms were still showing.

An ad connecting black fashion to Africa offers an interesting example of historical myth. In a September 2009 issue of *Harper's Bazaar* supermodel Naomi Campbell is in Africa photographed wearing animal print clothing. In one photo, she is racing a cheetah, in another she is jumping rope with monkeys, and in a third she is wrestling an alligator. The caption, "Wild Things" Oduok, 2009; Goodwin, 2014). H & M offered a hoodie that used the words "coolest monkey in the jungle" modeled by a young black boy,

A 2011 Nivea skincare for men ad was quickly pulled and the company apologized after comparing the image of a clean-shaven black man wearing a short, faded haircut to a decapitated head with a large bushy afro and a thick untrimmed mustache and beard. The message said, "Re-civilize Yourself" implying that the natural, thick, course, curly black hair was "uncivilized" (Ortiz, 2011).

Surprisingly, blackface is found in media depictions, especially ads more often than expected despite the fact that the image is known to be historically racist. It is part of America's racist past, and it is also a component of racialism (Brundage, 2011). *Bamboozled* a blackface satire written and directed by Spike Lee maintains a viable warning about what happens to black exploitation and problematic societal ideology when it is seen as acceptable (Clark, 2015).

Shoes under Katy Perry's name were designed resembling blackface, and Gucci's black turtle neck with a huge red circle around the lips brought a racist backlash (Ocbazghi and Skvaril, 2019; Blanchard, 2019). American Apparel clothing company used a woman in blackface with loud pink lips to promote their new clothing line suggesting, "Sweeter than Candy, Better than Cake" (Atlien, 2007). Dunkin Donuts released a Thailand ad for their chocolate donut that used a woman in blackface also with bright pink lips. The tag line read, "Charcoal Donut: Break Every Rule of Deliciousness" (Stanley, 2013). Blackface as an obvious part of the negative and painful minstrel era in American culture is racist.

There have been a number of heated debates concerning the issue of colorism in the media, particularly surrounding female celebrities whose skin has been lightened in certain advertisements. Colorism is included in the notion of racialism. Beyonce's skin color is obviously lighter in a 2008 L'Oreal ad campaign and Rihanna has been seen in various promotions with lighter skin (Paris, 2015). The cover of *Elle Magazine* was criticized for creating an image of Gabourey Sidibe with skin that looked lighter than her normal skin tone (Leach, 2010). Finally, Lupita Nyongo's beautiful, dark skin was lightened in a *Vanity Fair* layout (Wilson, 2014) and her response was to write a children's book, *Sulwe*, to help young black kids love themselves (Harper's Bazaar, 2018). The celebrity status of these black females connected to various beauty products is the basic purpose

Figure 3.2: Dunkin Donuts "Charcoal Donut" Ad in Thailand

of the ad, but the perpetuation of the myth of light skin as better than dark skin highlights and confirms the idea that light skin is closer to the accepted standard of white beauty.

Racialism is not always negative. Sometimes it is used to simply make a specific or symbolic point connected to race. For example, in some cases race has been associated with a product where the color of packaging or type of product is linked in some way with the race of the model. For example, Pantene recently launched a "strong and beautiful" campaign focused on African American hair. The new bottles of shampoo and conditioner are gold. But in the original campaign the Pantene bottles that were brown were displayed in ads with brown skinned women (Dan, 2017). In contrast, white women were shown in ads with white bottles of Pantene.

Figure 3.3: Cheerios "Interracial family" Super Bowl commercial

Life cereal released a series of racial ads. One depicted a young, black boy and girl on the front of their maple and brown sugar cereal box. While the regular box of Life Cereal displayed a white mother and child. Life's cinnamon flavored cereal boxes included a mix of black and white families.

The Cheerios ad in Figure 3.3 was immediately attacked when released. It is a contemporary and progressive representation of a bi-racial family and a two parent home. When this Cheerios ad first appeared in May of 2013 the primary focus was to sell Cheerios (Nudd, 2014). However, the story shows a mixed child pouring Cheerios on her black father's chest while he is sleeping. Earlier the mother had told the child that Cheerios were good for your heart. Despite the changing societal ideology about interracial relationships this ad touched on a taboo that is attached to such relationships in American culture which made it controversial (Goyette, 2013; Stump, 2013).

In July of 2015 Gerber launched an interesting ad campaign using a diversity of babies. The kids are enrolled in the college of chewing (Glammona, 2015). Each baby is sitting in a high chair eating Gerber products and wearing varsity jackets that reveal, "The Sport U chew logo." The caption that reads, "Earn your masters in chewing." This ad should be praised for its inclusiveness because the babies are obviously white, Asian, black and other ethnicities. However, in some of the photos the placement creates an adverse status. When the white baby is sitting in front of the Asian and black baby there is a hierarchy of importance suggesting an inferior or less than position.

Figure 3.4: Gerber "Earn your masters in chewing" problematic placement/status

It is also important to pay attention to how racial messages can be reframed to refocus a message. For example, the Pine-Sol ad below involves the reframing of a prominent black stereotype. The heavy black women, Diane Amos is responsible for cleaning which connects her to the mammy stereotype. However, that stereotype is literally turned upside down in this ad where Amos lays across the floor in a sexy pose wearing a satin robe, her make-up and hair done beautifully. She is depicted as the complete opposite of the mythical image of a mammy figure. Also, in an on-line commercial the Pine-Sol lady drives down an ocean road in her convertible and arrives at her mansion. Once she enters she finds rose petals on the stairs leading into the bedroom where a muscular, black man with no shirt on is mopping the bedroom floor. Again, an interesting alternative to the mammy stereotype (Edwards, 2010).

Finally, the use of Hip Hop and rap music in various advertising products has relevant implications for racialism. Rap music itself has been criticized as full of stereotypes and biased frames, so many of the adverting products that use rap music serve as good exemplars. One prominent example is the legend of the Dodge Brothers commercial. It is set in a high-class country club that begins to shake when a Dodge Durango drives by playing a heavy, beat-oriented rap song. The announcer says, "Well, there goes the country club" (Rohwedder, 2015). Even though the promotion is for the Dodge Durango you barely see the SUV pass by outside the window. Yet inside the club the elite, highbrow members show confusion. The rap song's pounding causes glasses to rattle, tables to shake and food to

Figure 3.5: Pine Sol "Intensity" reframing the mammy stereotype

tumble to the floor. The oppositional nature of rap music and black, urban, cool is contrasted with elite, privileged, country club behavior.

These are only a few of the exemplars that can be found in the world of advertising. There is a huge, shared cultural landscape of black stereotypes, biased frames, and historical myths tied to American media as well as images around the world. Advertising is constructed and negotiated as part of a negotiated communication process reflecting layers of meaning and perpetuating racialism. It is crucial for the creators of and consumers for advertising products to pay closer attention, especially when the images and messages involve black culture.

References

Atlien. (2007, August 24). Is the art? Model in blackface causes controversy. *Straight from the A*. Retrieved from http://straightfromthea.com/2007/08/24/is-this-art-model-in-blackface-causes-controversy/

Barthes, R. (1972). *Mythologies*. New York, NY: Hill and Wang.

Benetton Group. (1991). *Devil vs. Angel*. Retrieved from http://www.benettongroup.com/media-press/image-gallery/institutional-communication/historical-campaigns/

Blanchard, T. (2019, February 8). Courting controversy: From H&M's coolest monkey to Gucci's blackface jumper. *The Guardian*. Retrieved from https://www.theguardian.com/fashion/2019/feb/08/courting-controversy-from-hms-coolest-monkey-to-guccis-blackface-jumper

Brundage, F. (2011). *Beyond blackface: African Americans and the creation of American popular culture, 1890–1930*. Chapel Hill: University of North Carolina Press.

Burns, W. (2018, September 4). With new Kaepernick ad, what does Nike believe in? *Forbes*. Retrieved fromhttps://www.forbes.com/sites/willburns/2018/09/04/with-new-kaepernick-ad-what-does-nike-believe-in/#63b693a71081

Chambers, J. (2008). *Madison Avenue and the color line: African Americans in the advertising industry*. Philadelphia: University of Pennsylvania Press.

Clark, A. (2015, October 6). Bamboozled: Spike Lee's masterpiece on race in America is as relevant as ever. *The Guardian*. Retrieved from http://www.theguardian.com/film/2015/oct/06/bamboozled-spike-lee-masterpiece-race-in-america

Crocker, D. (2009, April–June). Marketing blackness: Using race to sell products. *Business and Economic Review, 55*(3), 6–9.

Dan, A. (2017, April 4). What marketers can learn from Pantene's stunning ode to black women. *Forbes*. Retrieved from https://www.forbes.com/sites/avidan/2017/04/04/what-marketers-can-learn-from-pantenes-stunning-ode-to-black-women/#5df254005cef

Dates, J., & Barlow, W. (1990). *Split image: African Americans and the media*. Washington, DC: Howard University Press.

Edwards, A., Edwards, C., Wahl, S., & Meyers, S. (2016). *The communication age: Connecting and engaging*. Thousand Oaks, CA: Sage.

Edwards, J. (2010, January 25). Is the new Pine-Sol ad racist? *CBS Moneywatch*. Retrieved from http://www.cbsnews.com/news/is-the-new-pine-sol-ad-racist/

Fontaine, S. (2009, October 1). Black Barbie doll portrayed as highly sexualized. *NEWSONE*. Retrieved from https://newsone.com/534165/black-barbie-doll-portrayed-as-highly-sexualized/

Gibbs, A. (2016, October 4). Chance the Rapper gives voice to new Kit Kat jingle. *Forbes*. Retrieved from https://www.forbes.com/sites/adriennegibbs/2016/10/04/chance-the-rapper-in-new-kit-kat-commercial/#40c9d07968c7

Glammona, C. (2015, April 30). Gerber tries to cure picky eating with chunkier food. *Bloomberg Business*. Retrieved from http://www.bloomberg.com/news/articles/2015-04-30/gerber-engineers-chunkier-baby-food-to-stave-off-picky-eating

Goodwin, C. C. (2014, February 11). Harpers Bazaar—Wild Thing editorial. *LCA Critical Journal*. Retrieved from https://cgcriticaljournal.wordpress.com/2014/02/11/harpers-bazaar-wild-thing-editorial/

Goyette, B. (2013, May 31). Cheerios commercial featuring mixed-race family gets racist backlash. *Huffpost Business*. Retrieved from http://www.huffingtonpost.com/2013/05/31/cheerios-commercial-racist-backlash_n_3363507.html

Harper's Bazaar staff. (2018, January 18). Lupita Nyong'o to publish children's book tackling skin lightening. Harper's Bazaar. Retrieved from https://www.harpersbazaar.com/uk/culture/culture-news/a15384073/lupita-nyongo-childrens-book-skin-lightening/

Jones, V. (2017, December 6). "Black people "loot" food, white people "find" food. *Huffpost Politics*. Retrieved from http://www.huffingtonpost.com/van-jones/black-people-loot-food-wh_b_6614.html

Leach, B. (2010, September 16). *Elle Magazine* in Gabourey Sidibe skin lightening controversy. *The Telegraph*. Retrieved from http://www.telegraph.co.uk/news/celebrity news/8005734/Elle-magazine-in-Gabourey-Sidibe-skin-lightening-controversy.html

Nudd, T. (2014, January 29). Ad of the day: Cheerios brings back its famous interracial family for the Super Bowl. *Adweek*. Retrieved from http://www.adweek.com/news/advertising-branding/ad-day-cheerios-brings-back-its-famous-interracial-family-super-bowl-155302

Ocbazghi, E. and Skvaril, C. (2019, February 27). Why these Gucci clothes are racist. *Business insider*. Retrieved from https://www.businessinsider.com/why-gucci-clothes-racist-blackface-sambo-2019-2

Oduok, U. (2009, August 14). Naomi Campbell "Wild Things" Harper's Bazaar shoot offensive? *Ladybrille Magazine*. Retrieved from https://ladybrille.com/naomi-campbell-wild-things-harpers-bazaar-shoot-offensive/

Ortiz, J. (2011, August 19). Nivea pull racist "recivilize yourself" ad after sparking outrage. *Business Insider*. Retrieved from https://www.businessinsider.com/nivea-racist-recivilize-yourself-ad-2011-8

Paris, M. (2015, October 23). Why do so many of my fellow black stars want whiter skin? *Daily Mail*. Retrieved from http://www.dailymail.co.uk/tvshowbiz/article-3286969/As-Beyonce-steps-palest-shade-MICA-PARIS-asks-black-stars-want-whiter-skin.html

Rohwedder, K. (2015, June 26). What's the song in the Dodge Durango commercial? It's no flex zone and it's terrific. *Bustle.com*. Retrieved from http://www.bustle.com/articles/93204-whats-the-song-in-the-dodge-durango-commercial-its-no-flex-zone-its-terrific-videos

Schneider, M. (2009, August 30). NBC to get more colorful. *Variety*. Retrieved from https://variety.com/2009/tv/news/nbc-to-get-more-colorful-1118007883/

Stanley, T. L. (2013, September 3). Dunkin' Donuts apologizes for blackface ad, but not everyone is sorry. *Adweek*. Retrieved from http://www.adweek.com/adfreak/dunkin-donuts-apologizes-blackface-ad-not-everyone-sorry-152172

Stump, S. (2013, June 3). Cheerios ad with mixed-race family draws racists responses. *Today News*. Retrieved from http://www.today.com/news/cheerios-ad-mixed-race-family-draws-racist-responses-6C10169988

United Colors of Benetton. (2013). Controversial Ad Lab. Retrieved from https://controadlab.tumblr.com/post/49708405724/devil-vs-angel-united-colors-of

Wilson, J. (2014, January 16). *Vanity Fair* accused of lightening Lupita Nyongo's skin color, do you agree? *Huffington Post*. Retrieved from http://www.huffingtonpost.com/2014/01/16/vanity-fair-lupita-nyongo-skin-lightening_n_4608954.html

Yang, L. (2018, May 2). This photo of a Black Barbie doll's hairstyle is dividing the internet – and some feel it fails to represent how black women actually style their hair. *Insider*. Retrieved from https://www.insider.com/black-barbie-doll-hair-controversy-2018-5

CHAPTER FOUR

Black-ish and the Changing Nature of Black Identity

Black-ish has proven to be a very successful black situation comedy. The show won a number of awards including several NAACP Image Awards, the AFI TV program of the year, the Television Critics Association Award for Outstanding Achievement in Comedy, a Peabody Award for Entertainment and Children's Programming, plus Tracee Ellis Ross won a Golden Globe for Best Actress in a Television Series—Musical or Comedy (*Black-ish*, 2017).

The storyline explores the struggle that many black people experience in order to maintain their sense of culture while at the same time progressing in the American mainstream. This chapter investigates how certain representations and narratives in *Black-ish* are designed to deconstruct the changing perspectives surrounding blackness and authenticity. *Black-ish* offers a look at how black identity operates in direct opposition to the signification of white identity in American society. This analysis provides a relevant examination of black culture's changing role and meaning in the 21st century.

In the media, various notions of blackness are perpetuated through commodified products. For example, there are black cable channels like *BET, TV ONE*, and *Centric* that primarily play programs with a black focus. There are popular television and film producers like Shonda Rhimes and Tyler Perry who create films and television shows with leading black characters. In the music industry Beyonce's message album "Lemonade" won an Oscar for best urban contemporary album (McDermott, 2017), while Common and John Legend's award winning collaboration on the song "Glory" for the historic movie *Selma* was also praised (Newman, 2015).

The purpose of this chapter is to think about the function of the hit ABC television show *Black-ish* as it explores the authenticity of blackness. This show offers a critique of race and culture through key sites of struggle for the black family at home, work, and school. How does racialism work through the narrative of *Black-ish* with the deconstruction of selected stereotypes, biased frames, and historic myths?

Black Identity and Authenticity

Research on racial identity and authenticity is relevant to this examination. Davis and Gandy (1999) define racial identity as an ideological organizing mechanism. They suggest that racial identity is shaped by social contexts, including media images and messages. Within African American culture difference is recognized through social contexts as influential to black identity (Gandy 2001). In other words, black identity is shaped by a difference in cultural background, values, and belief systems.

According to Nguyen and Anthony (2014) authenticity involves the signification of what is accepted as real and true.

> We broadly define Black authenticity as a cultural resource legitimized through ideologies, actions and interactions. Black authenticity includes ideals and expectations that affects what it means to 'be Black' in relation to personal, public and cultural identities. (p. 770)

In their research, Nguyen and Anthony argue that blackness is a shifting and changing notion based on two processes. First, the commodification of realness as part of black authenticity created in the process of controlling images. Second, the legitimization of memberships defined as personal and group identity construction.

What is considered legitimately black is constantly changing and those changes ultimately impact black identity. Davis and Gandy (1999) believe that racial identity plays a powerful role in how we respond to the mass media. They argue that social experience is shaped by everyday interactions, values, norms, beliefs, and morals, which means racial identity can shape behavior and choice as it relates to the popular ideal in mass media.

> Racial identity may be understood as an ideological position. In its most general sense, ideology is defined as 'pattern of ideal, belief systems, or interpretive schemes' found in a society or among specific social groups. (p. 368)

It is also important to note that social identity is learned and it is always multidimensional (Bussell & Crandall, 2002; Berry 1998, 2000). Gender, class, race, nationality, religion, and other considerations make up identification criteria. These categories can enable communities and cultures to come together based on shared experience (Cross, Parham, & Helms, 1991).

> The term Nigrescence is derived from French and means 'to become Black'. It seeks to explain and measure the process through which African American adults are transformed into persons who are more Afrocentric. (p. 374)

The strength of black authenticity and the modification of black identity are evident throughout the sitcom *Black-ish*. As Nuguyen and Anthony (2014) suggest, often through these kinds of commodified images identity is negotiated to fit in or it is distinguished to ultimately influence the presentation of an authentic self.

Deconstruction Theory and Semiotics

Norris asks in his 2004 book on deconstruction how language can be at once the most rigorous, and the most unreliable source of knowledge. "Deconstruction works at the same giddy limit, suspending all that we take for granted about language, experience and the normal possibilities of human communication." (p. xii)

Deconstruction theory was first introduced by Derrida (1976). Based on his writing in literature and philosophy, he believed that texts were meant to be undone, criticized, and even revised. Derrida took on both the written and spoken word in his writings. Norris also explains that all forms of writing offer perplexities of meaning and intent, but voice is an important metaphor of truth and authenticity.

> deconstruction is not simply a strategic reversal of categories which otherwise remain distinct and unaffected. It seeks to undo both a given order of priorities and the very system of conceptual opposition that make that order possible. (p. 31)

Culler (2007) argues that deconstruction theory works with postmodern and poststructuralist thinking to inspire suspicion and skepticism. He suggests that during its diffusion into the humanities and social sciences, deconstruction in the broadest sense became a critique of categories taken as natural and a drive to pursue the analysis of the logic of signification in a given area.

According to Turner (2016), deconstruction is the ongoing process of questioning meaning.

> Finally, deconstruction is not an act or an operation. Rather, it is something that happens, something that takes place. It takes place everywhere. It does not require deliberation or consciousness, but rather its potential exists within our structures of meaning. It is interested in exploring and revealing the internal logic of ideas and meaning. It is concerned with opening up these structures and revealing the way in which our understanding of foundational concepts is constructed. (p. 4)

Finally, the notion of "differance" used by Bennington and Derrida (1993) posits meaning as not fixed or static. According to Tyrus (1999) "differance" is based on a normal process of negotiation constantly competing and evolving. In *Positions* (1981), Derrida looks at deconstruction in the creation of opposition and the search for new meanings. As a matter of fact, deconstruction was developed in opposition to structuralism and as proposed by Saussure and Barthes led to a new science of signs called semiotics.

Semiotics involves the basic understanding of the signifier or text, along with the signified representation. Or as explained by Barthes (1983), first interpret the basic information or images (signifier), then analyze the meaning of that representation (signified). In his semiological approach, Barthes uses three types of signification. The denotative sign which is the basic representation, the connotative or expressive connection to that sign, and third any myth or ideology that has also been attached to the sign.

According to Bouzida (2014), the media are an important part of our life and semiology is a good approach to understanding and decoding the significant messages used by the media to generate meanings for sociocultural and personal associations. The deconstruction of racial signifiers through *Black-ish* offers a valuable opportunity to better understand how structural signs and symbols can be questioned and even redefined. In other words, the "differance" in language and visual images presented in the show are not value-free.

Changing Black Identity and Reassessing Black Authenticity

So, what is black authenticity and how is it different from black identity? That is the important question explored in the popular situation comedy *Blackish*. The show features a successful black family living in the suburbs. The father Dre is an advertising executive, the mother Rainbow (Bow) is an anesthesiologist and they have five kids.

The show focuses directly on how blackness is changing in the Johnson family. Three generations of black cultural ideas are dissected and critiqued as part of the transformation that this family experiences on a weekly basis. The deconstruction of exemplars from a fundamental narrative like *Black-ish* provides a good look at how black identity is changing.

Exemplars have been selected from all three seasons. It is interesting to note that even episode titles demonstrate resistance and transformation connected to black identity. For example, the season three episodes examined are; "ToysRn'tUs," "Lemons," and "Who's Afraid of the Big Black Man?"—the season two episodes are; "The Word," "Rock, Paper, Scissors, Gun," and "Dr. Hell No,"—the season one episodes are; "The Pilot," "The Nod," and "Black Santa/White Christmas."

Season 1, Episode 1 "Pilot"

Dre in a voiceover describes his life as a kid from the hood and admits that he is now living the American dream. He is an educated black man worried that when brothers start getting a little money things can get a little weird. There is a shot of the Johnson family standing in front of their suburban home when a tour bus drives by. The family waves to the people on the bus as the tour guide says," If you look to your left you'll see the mythical and majestic black family out of their natural habitat, and still thriving." This is the first explanation of the show's ultimate purpose, to challenge and in some cases dismiss the stereotype of a broken black family living in poverty. The symbolism of a zoo through framing plays into the historical myth of the African diaspora. Dre continues his voiceover below.

> Sometimes I worry that in an effort to make it black folks have dropped a little bit their culture, and the rest of the world has picked it up. They even renamed it urban, and in the urban world Justin Timberlake and Robin Thicke are R & B gods, Kim Kardashian is the symbol for big butts and Asian guys are just unholdable on the dance floor. Come on! Big butts, R & B, and dancing those were the black mans go tos.

The oldest son Junior's lack of blackness becomes a conflict between Dre and Bow in this episode. Junior wants to play field hockey and Dre is upset. He dismisses Bow's support for her son's choice by telling Bow that she is not really black anyway. He calls her bi-racial, mixed, and omni-colored complexioned (Bow's mother is black and her father is white). Bow responds, "If I'm not really black could somebody please tell my hair and my ass." This response is a good example of the many symbols of blackness used throughout the show to suggest authenticity.

A black woman's hair is thick and course, and her behind is often big not like the typical standard image of white beauty. So, Bow uses these elements to assure her husband that she is the real thing.

Later in the episode, when Junior wants to convert to Judaism because he thinks a bar mitzvah is a party, Dre instead pulls together a special African "Rights of Passage" ceremony for his son's sixteenth birthday. Dre and Junior are dressed in African attire in the backyard surrounded by African drums, chairs covered in Kente cloth, and woven baskets. Junior holds a rain stick while Dre rubs brown paint across his son's forehead, then blows a white substance in his face. When they are caught by Bow the ceremony ends.

Dre eventually compromises by throwing his son a Hip Hop Bro-mitzvah. This party has obvious associations with several black stereotypes such as Dre and Junior's matching urban style sweat suits, large gold chains, and white, designer tennis shoes. Rap music plays loudly while friends laugh, dance, eat, and enjoy the celebration of negotiating blackness.

Season 1, Episode 10 "Black Santa/White Christmas"

The episode starts with a voiceover by Dre: "I love Christmas … Santa was the first white man I ever loved." The storyline is about Dre's excitement when he has the opportunity to play Santa Clause at the office party for needy families. At home Dre tells his own family that most of the kids, who are mainly minorities, have only seen Santa as some random white guy. This is his chance to show them that Santa can look just like them.

Diane:	How can Santa look like a kid? Santa looks like Santa.
Dre:	Of course baby, Santa looks like Santa.
Bow:	Because there's only one Santa, but Daddy want to be one of Santa's helpers. Isn't that nice?"
Diane:	But we'll still get our presents from the real Santa right?
Jack:	The white one?

Dre and Bow are obviously bothered by their twin's limited notion of Santa. This idea that Santa is white and he has all the power when it comes to gift giving is a racial signifier that Dre is determined to challenge. But because a white female in the office was passed over for Santa, she sets out to ruin things. She doesn't tell Dre that he is supposed to secure presents for the kids, so there are no presents at the event. And when the kids discover there are no gifts, one child mumbles" "No toys. This never happened with white Santa." The salient bias against a black Santa posed at work and at home ties closely to the idea of what is real or authentic. A certain race and/or color seems to be necessary to maintain the norm despite Dre's enthusiasm and desire to change things.

Season 1, Episode 23 "Elephant in the Room"

When Dre and Bow find out that their oldest son, Andre Junior has joined the Young Republicans club at school they panic.

Bow:	We don't do that Dre. We are compassionate liberals who believe in tolerance and acceptance …
Dre:	(interrupts her) Yeah, whatever, Bow. We're black. That's all that matters.
	And later in the conference room at work:
Dre:	You can't be a black republican. They are not down for us, so we are not down for them."
Charlie:	(Dre's black colleague) Dre, you've got to do something about Junior. You don't want him to end up an Uncle Tom."
Mr. Stevens:	(Dre's white boss) Why not? I loved my Uncle Tom. Okay, he wasn't actually my Uncle Tom, but he was a great, black guy named Jim. He worked for my dad, and did everything he was told even at the expense of his own community. (hesitates) Being an Uncle Tom isn't a great thing is it?

Dre's boss has bought into the stereotype. This scene exposes how such a biased frame can be called out. The signification of white identity is effectively deconstructed.

Season 1, Episode 3 "The Nod"

The episode starts with Dre's voiceover explaining how important it is for two black men to nod in respect when passing each other. Dre gets upset when he witnesses Junior not following this black tradition. According to Dre, it is a tradition that is important to all real black men, even the first black president. We watch as two mothers on one side of the sidewalk and one mother on the other side pass each other pushing their children down the street in strollers. As the two black male kids pass each other they toss their heads up into the air in a respectful nod. This scene is humorous since both kids are too young to know what they are doing, yet they do it anyway. Later in the Johnson kitchen, Bow begs Dre not to make it a big deal.

Bow:	Dre please do not turn this into yet another thing. The truth is that Junior's generation has a different opinion on the struggle than you and pops. Can't you just let that be a good thing?
Dre:	No! Bow, the nod is on the same primal level as a baby waving hi.
Pops:	That's right.
Dre:	As a man scrunching up his face when a woman with a big butt walks by, whew!
Pops:	(shivers) Ahhhhh.

This conversation circles back to an earlier stereotype by Dre about how black women are being pushed out of the big butt category by white women like Kim Kardashian. Yet, Dre and his father share a moment of admiration for black women's behinds challenging that loss and showing that ideologically they remain supportive.

Season 2, Episode 1 "The Word"

This episode tackles the n-word. In a school talent show Dre's younger son Jack sings "Gold Digger" by Kanye West which includes the n-word. His performance is cut short, and he is threatened with suspension from school. At work the n-word discussion moves through the various labels like Black, African American, and Colored, ending in a satirical narrative that questions the NAACP's use of the word colored today. At home Zoey tells Dre that her friends say the n-word all the time so it's not a big deal.

Dre:	Which friends?
Zoey:	Dillon, Asher, and Jacob.
Ruby:	(Dre's mother) Oh honey, those sound like white boys. Don't you know any Tyrones, or Kelvans or maybe a nice Nashawn.
Zoey:	Oh, I do know a Tyrone, but he's in Jail.
Ruby:	Yeah, that can happen to a Tyrone.
Dre:	Why do you let your friends say it?
Zoey:	It's not like they mean anything by it. It's just a word.
Dre:	I can't believe this. My generation fought to take that word back while your sexting, insta-dumy generation is giving it away to everybody ... he (the white man) either wants nobody to say it because he can't or everybody to say it because he wants to ... My son should be able to say the n-word to his heart's content, and Asher should never be able to say it.

There is a significant racial connection to the word demonstrated by Dre while his oldest daughter Zoey displays no such link. This generational divide within the black community is confronted and questioned as Dre is adamant that reclaiming power over the n-word is connected to real blackness.

Season 2, Episode 2 "Rock, Paper, Scissors, Gun"

When there is a break-in down the street from the Johnson's, Dre wants to buy a gun for protection. Bow is against it and a conflict ensues. Bow explains that every day at the hospital she sees what guns do to people. Dre argues that they need a gun for safety. He needs to be able to protect his family.

Dre eventually ignores Bow and goes to the gun shop anyway. He asks the clerk for a handgun that he can hold sideways like he's seen in the movies. When he buys the gun, and takes it home Bow stops speaking to him. Then late one night they hear someone bumbling around downstairs in the house. The kids hear it too, so they run into their parent's room afraid. Bow tells Dre to get the gun. The gun is still in the box, and Dre can't get the box open. As the footsteps get closer everyone panics and suddenly, the door swings open wide. Dre shoves his hand in the box pointing it at his father who has obviously been drinking and stumbles into the room.

This episode was constructed to address stereotypical images and messages about blacks, violence, and guns. There are some biased frames like when Dre holds the gun straight out and sideways as if he is a gangsta. But, for the most part, the primary message is that not all black people are violent, and many don't own or use guns. There are two oppositional black perspectives from each parent. And the final frame leaves everyone questioning the stereotypes concerning blacks, guns and violence.

Season 2, Episode 16 "Hope"

The Johnson family watches television together as a court case dealing with police brutality is decided. When the court finds that the police officer will not face a grand jury, Zoey feels hopeless about the future. Dre explains to his family that the world we live in is a whole lot of white and a whole lot of black, but mostly gray.

Ruby: (Dre's mother) I cannot believe this keeps happening.
Pops: (Dre's father) I can't believe you're surprised it keeps happening.
Bow: I know it's bad you guys, but despite it's flaws we still have the best justice system in the whole world. We just have to have faith that it is going to work itself out.

Dre:	And why should we listen to you again Bow, when you just assured us that these men would be brought to justice.
Bow:	Because I hoped that they would.
Dre:	Why Bow, when has it ever worked for us? When do we ever get a win?
Bow:	How about O.J.?
Pops:	There it is!
Ruby:	That's low even for you Rainbow.
Dre:	No mom, no, not at all. This is actually a perfect example. It shows how black people were so desperate for a win that we had to root for this idiot.
Bow:	I'm just trying for the sake of our children to find a silver lining here. Let's not forget that statistically speaking the system works more than it doesn't.
Diane:	(looking at her phone) Well, according to these statistics, 25% of police shootings in L.A. county from 2010 to 2014 were of unarmed suspects.
Jack:	What? The police are shooting people with no arms? Why am I just now hearing this?
Junior:	No Jack unarmed means he didn't have a weapon.
Jack:	Of course he didn't have a weapon, he had no arms.

By exposing the real nature of black frustration as it relates to the police, this scene exemplifies the deconstruction of white norms and black stereotypes. The statistics are cited as a way to empower blackness and solidify authenticity and when the Johnson family shares their values and experiences it can negate the frustrating ideas found in certain biased frames.

Season 3, Episode 4 "Who's Afraid of the Big Black Man"

Dre is driving his drunk, white, female neighbor home in her car along with Junior, and Bow's brother, Yohan. Because he was just going up the street, Dre left his wallet at home. Of course, he gets stopped by the police. Dre thinks through possible scenarios as he waits for the police officer to approach the car. In one scenario, he tells the police officer that the car belongs to the passed out white lady in the passenger seat, and there is a jump to the scene where a jail door slams shut with Dre inside the cell. Another scenario shows Dre warning the officer that he is going to videotape the encounter, we hear a gunshot, and this time the jump is to Dre's funeral. Eventually Dre opens the car door and starts running with the song "Straight Outta Compton" playing in the background.

This scene demonstrates how many black males in America believe that this kind of situation with the police could lead to a negative outcome. Racial bias among police officers is constructed as a problem and Dre is overwhelmed with fear. This episode makes the point that extreme measures are sometimes taken by police officers and black men often run out of fear. Dre not only jumps out of the car and takes off, but he leaves his sixteen-year-old son in the back seat along with his brother in law. Later, when Dre learns that Junior ran too. They hug, and Dre tells him that he is proud.

Season 3, Episode 12 "Lemons"

This episode takes place after the 2016 election, Dre offers up a powerful monologue concerning the struggle of black people in America when he is accused of not caring about this country because he doesn't show enough outrage for the election results.

> You don't think I care about this country. I love this country even though at times it doesn't love me back. For my whole life, my parents, my grandparents, me, for most black people this system has never worked for us. But we still played ball, tried to do our best to live by the rules even though we knew they would never work out in our favor. We had to live in neighborhoods that you wouldn't drive through, send our kids to school with books so beat up you couldn't read 'em, worked jobs that you wouldn't even consider in your nightmares. Black people wake up every day believing that our lives are going to change, even though everything around us says its not. Truth be told, you ask most black people and they tell you that no matter who won the election they didn't expect the hood to get better. But they still voted because that's what you're supposed to do. You think I'm not sad that Hillary didn't win, that I'm not terrified about what Trump's about to do. I'm used to things not going my way ... I love this country as much if not more than you do and don't you ever forget that.

During Dre's monologue the song "Strange Fruit" by Billie Holiday plays, and we see images of "For colored only" signs, trash in schools, graffiti on walls, and a church choir singing. At the end of the scene Dre storms out of the room, and the song ends.

In this monologue Dre uses the history of black culture in America to confirm his love for his country. He demonstrates his rage, often a stereotype for black men, while his colleagues, black and white, male and female show an obvious discomfort. The conference room of Dre's workplace is consistently designated as a place where social, cultural, and racial issues can be discussed openly.

Season 3, Episode 17 "ToysRn'tUs"

Bow Johnson tackles the inequality in pop culture when Diane is given a white doll for her birthday. Bow takes the white doll back to the store to exchange it for a black doll. The store is called *Girl Story*, and there are hundreds of white dolls representing doctors, pilots, and teachers, but there are only two black dolls in the store. One is a run-away slave, and the other is a protest marcher with an afro.

Bow blows up because of the limited choices when it comes to the representation of black culture. She organizes a protest where several white dolls are burned while Diane hides behind a sign that says "Black Toys Matter." Later at home, Bow explains to Dre that the images that their kids see affect who they are and who they aspire to become.

In the same episode another key issue of blackness is tackled as Dre develops a successful campaign for a company called Boxable. He presents a white family; father, mother and two kids holding up Boxable boxes. Each box is a different size matching the family member. For example, the youngest holds the smallest box. The tag line for the ad is "Boxable: The Gold Standard." When Dre's boss tells him that the ad is perfect because "The Gold Standard" means success, dependability, and shirts tucked into pants, Dre decides to find a black family who can also represent "The Gold Standard." He tells his colleagues that white is always the default unless someone chooses to move the ball forward. He plans to be that someone. Dre recasts the ad with a black family, but he is chastised because the chosen family is light skinned. The issue of colorism is explored here because this is not the first time that Dre has chosen a black family with light skin for an ad.

This storyline addresses two major issues in black culture concerning black identity and authenticity (Fujioka, 2005; Martin, 2008). First, it is important to Bow that her children know who they are and she wants to surround them with images that empower black culture. Second, Dre realizes that his preference for light skin is problematic because of the historical myth that light skinned blacks are better than or preferred over dark-skinned blacks. This historical myth has survived since slavery when white men raped black female slaves. The mixed children born from these adverse unions often worked in the house separated from the darker skinned blacks who worked in the fields often causing tension.

As a popular sitcom, *Black-ish* exemplifies the struggle to redefine blackness in the twenty-first century. It has been praised for its examination of racial transformation (Bianco, 2014; Genzlinger, 2014; Piccalo, 2016). Stereotypes, biased frames, and historical myths can shape notions of black identity and authenticity.

Many of the images and messages in *Black-ish* are contextualized within the larger society offering a significant illustration of how black identity has been forced to change.

Racial signifiers in each episode help to spark a conversation about the daily struggles experienced by black people such as a fear of the police by black men, the need for positive black representation, the importance of black history, and the power of white privilege. These conversations are used to better understand how changes operate in such black cultural contexts like the Black Lives Matter movement (Ryan, 2016). Racial identity is usually shaped by social contexts such as white accommodation and black identification in the media (Cooper, 2001; Stevenson, 2009). Erickson (1995) has suggested that black identity and authenticity as a cultural product also tends to reflect black commodification.

> Much like identities, feelings of authenticity are grounded in meaning. Yet, the meanings referred to in one's system of self values do more than lend substance to particular role-identities … Because some self-values are more important to one's sense of authenticity than others, they may help to explain the range of commitments we hold to particular role identities (134).

It is Dre's self-values that push his efforts to maintain at least part of his blackness. The importance of authenticity for Dre is based on expectations and negotiation. According to Nguyen and Anthony (2014), although blackness can be commodified it can only be legitimized by individual actions and interactions. Yet, Culler (2007) argues that deconstruction in today's postmodern and poststructural society inspires suspicion and skepticism when it comes to "differance." *Black-ish*, is a humorous narrative about how black culture is changing. It delivers a weekly storyline that is meant to criticize and transform "difference" as an important part of racialism.

References

Barthes, R. (1983). *The Barthes Reader*. New York, NY: Hill and Wang.
Bennington, G., & Derrida, J. (1993). *Jacques Derrida*. Chicago, IL: University of Chicago Press.
Berry, G. L. (1998). Black family life on television and the socialization of the African American child: Images of marginality. *Journal of Comparative Family Studies, 29*, 233–242.
Berry, G. L. (2000). Multicultural media portrayals and the changing demographic landscape: The psychosocial impact of television representations on the adolescent of color. *Journal of Adolescent Health, 27*(Suppl.), 57–60.
Blackish Awards. Retrieved from http://www.imdb.com/title/tt3487356/awards

Bianco, R. (2014, September 23). *ABC's Black-ish* explores subtle shades on racial issues. *USA Today*. Retrieved from http://www.usatoday.com/story/life/tv/2014/09/23/blackish-review/16105525/

Bouzida, F. (2014, September 8–10). *The semiology analysis in media studies: Roland Barthes approach*. International Conference on Social Sciences and Humanities, pp. 1001–1007.

Bussell, R., & Crandall, H. (2002). Television viewing and perceptions about race differences in socioeconomic success. *Journal of Broadcasting and Electronic Media, 46*, 265–282.

Cooper, G. (2001, Summer). Television and social identity: Race representation as "white" accommodation. *Journal of Broadcasting and Electronic Media, 45*(3), 413–431.

Cross, W. Jr., Parham, T., & Helms, J. (1991). The stages of black identity development: Nigrescence models. In R. L. Jones (ed.), *Black psychology* (pp. 319–338). Berkley, CA: Cobb & Henry.

Culler, J. (2007). *On Deconstruction: Theory and criticism after structuralism*. New York, NY: Cornell University Press.

Davis, J., & Gandy, O. (1999, January). Racial identity and media orientation: Exploring the nature of constraint. *Journal of Black Studies, 29*(3), 367–397.

Derrida, J. (1981). *Positions*. London, England: The Athlone Press.

Erickson, R. (1995). The importance of authenticity for self and society. *Symbolic Interaction, 18* (2), 121–144.

Fujioka, Y. (2005). Black media images as a perceived threat to African American ethnic identity: Coping responses, perceived public perception, and attitudes towards affirmative action. *Journal of Broadcasting & Electronic Media, 49*, 450–467.

Gandy, O. H. (2001). Racial identity, media use, and the social construction of risk among African Americans. *Journal of Black Studies, 31*(5), 600–618.

Genzlinger, N. (2014, September 23). A family rooted in two realms: *Black-ish* a new ABC comedy taps racial issues. *The New York Times*. Retrieved from https://www.nytimes.com/2014/09/24/arts/television/black-ish-a-new-abc-comedy-taps-racial-issues.html?_r=0

Martin, A. C. (2008). Television media as a potential negative factor in racial identity development of African American youth. *Academic Psychiatry, 32*(4), 338–342.

Mastro, D., & Greenberg, B. (2000). The portrayal of racial minorities on prime-time television. *Journal of Broadcasting and Electronic Media, 44*(4), 690–703.

Mastro, D. E., & Tropp, L. R. (2004). The effects of interracial contact, attitudes and stereotypical portrayals on evaluations of black television sitcom characters. *Communication Research Reports, 21*, 119–129.

McDermott, M. (2017, February 14). Why Beyonce's Lemonade lost the grammys and why she should have won. *USA Today*. Retrieved from http://www.usatoday.com/story/life/music/2017/02/13/why-beyonce-lemonade-lost-the-grammys-why-she-should-have-won/97847070/

Newman, J. (2015). Glory wins best original song at Oscars, brings cast to tears. *Rolling Stone*. Retrieved from https://www.rollingstone.com/music/music-news/glory-wins-best-original-song-at-oscars-brings-cast-to-tears-119428/

Nguyen, J., & Anthony, A. (2014). Black authenticity: Defining the ideas and expectations in the construction of real blackness. *Sociology Compass, 8*(6), 770–778.

Norris, C. (2004). *Deconstruction: Theory and practice.* New York, NY: Routledge

Piccalo, G. (2016, May 18). *Black-ish* looks to get the tough issues out in the open. The *Los Angeles Times.* Retrieved from http://www.latimes.com/entertainment/ envelope/la-en-st-0519-blackish-cast-20160510-snap-story.html

Ryan, M. (2016, February 23). *Black-ish* is the ideal sitcom for the age of black lives matter. *Variety.* Retrieved from http://variety.com/2016/tv/features/black-ish-abc-kenya-barris-anthony-anderson-1201711794/

Stevenson, H. C., & Arrington, E. G. (2009, April). Racial socialization mediates the relationship between perceived racism and racial identity among African American adolescents. Cultural Diversity and Ethnic Minority Psychology. *Special issue from the Study Group on Race, Culture and Ethnicity (NIMH), 15*(2), 125–136.

Turner, C. (2016, May 27). Jacques Derrida: Deconstruction. *Critical Legal Thinking.* Retrieved from http://criticallegalthinking.com/2016/05/27/jacques-derrida-deconstruction/

Tyrus, J. (1999). Difference as the norm: An interpretive study of the audience for black sitcoms on the *WP* and *UPN* Networks. Dissertation, Ohio University.

CHAPTER FIVE

Balancing Stereotypes: Black Male and Female Roles on Prime-Time Television

Shonda Rhimes is one of the most prominent prime-time writers and producers on the small screen. Her successful shows have dominated Thursday nights on *ABC* for more than a decade. This includes, *Grey's Anatomy* (2005–), *Private Practice* (2007–2013), *Scandal* (2012–2018), *How to Get Away with Murder* (2014–), and *Station 19* (2018–). Shondaland's move to Netflix in 2018 included the freedom to develop eight new shows under a nine-figure deal (Koblin, 2018).

In a 2018 *Elle Magazine* interview, Rhimes explained that the one thing she knew she wanted to do in her television shows was to represent everybody so that each episode looked like the real world.

> … I was inducted into the Television Academy Hall of Fame. I was trying to figure out my speech, and I realized how it was about how you cannot be what you cannot see. I talked about having grown up watching Oprah every single day of my life. How this was a woman of color who did not look a certain way, who was [based] in Chicago, and who took over the world through television basically.

Rhimes has created complex television images, especially when it comes to black women. Olivia Pope in *Scandal*, Annalise Keating in *How to get Away with Murder*, and Miranda Bailey in *Grey's Anatomy* each depicting a complicated black protagonist that helps to balance out black female stereotypes like the Jezebel, the mammy, and the angry black woman.

There are also a number of black male characters who provide a balancing act on prime-time television, particularly related to narratives surrounding the criminal justice system. Black authority figures can be an effective way to resist the barrage of black male stereotypes such as criminals, gang bangers, thugs, and drug dealers. For example, in *Law and Order Special Victims Unit* (1999–) Ice T is featured as Sergeant Odafin Tutuola, *NCIS Los Angeles* (2009–) includes Sam Hanna played by LL Cool J, Shemar Moore stars as Daniel Hondo Harrelson in *SWAT* (2017–), and newcomer Morris Chestnut, plays an FBI agent Will Keaton on *The Enemy Within* (2019–).

These prime-time images are relevant because the television set is the most important catalyst for representation in most American households. Approximately 80 percent of Americans watch television on any given day (Krantz-Kent, 2018). Research has reported that African Americans watch linear television and also stream television shows more than any other group (Umstead, 2018).

A 2017 Neilson study found that on average African Americans consume up to 13 hours of media a day. That same study also suggested that television shows with predominantly black casts or a black leading character draws substantial non-black viewers. One table demonstrated that in 2016–2017 the audience for Rhimes's hit shows *How to Get Away with Murder* and *Scandal* were 69 and 68 percent non-black respectively (Neilson Insights, 2017).

Black Stereotypes

Black stereotypes of the 1800s have been consistently perpetuated through film and television (Toll, 1974). Mammy, Jezebel, Sambo, Coon, Buck, Uncle Tom, and Aunt Jemima were the norm when it came to black representations in American culture (Bogle, 2016; Turner, 2002). In 2000, Mastro and Greenberg studied black roles on television during the 1996–1997 season and reported that approximately 16 percent of major and minor roles were black images, but most were negative. They also found that many of those black characters were featured on early police shows as criminals. For example, shows like *NYPD Blue* (1993), *Cops* (1989), and *New York Undercover* (1994).

In 2010, Monk-Turner, Heiserman, and others studied television and suggested that things had improved just a little. African Americans were three times more likely than Latinos to appear on prime-time television, but still primarily in minor roles with mixed messages. For example, they noted that some black and Latino characters were depicted as less intelligent and some were considered more intelligent, however they found that black characters for the most part were usually in more despicable, immoral, and less respected roles.

Substantial research has studied how stereotypes continue to influence American society through the media (Brown-Givens & Monahan, 2005; Entman & Rojecki, 2001; Harris-Perry, 2011; Jewell, 1993; Mastro, 2017; Plous & Williams, 1995; Punyanunt-Carter, 2008). And of course, Gerbner's Cultivation Theory (Gerbner, Gross & others, 2002) can help explain how television impacts society's view of the world. Specifically, Gerbner found that heavy television viewers tend to believe in the kind of world presented by the shows that they watch (Vrij, 1996; Weigel, Kim, & Frost, 1995). This means that when stereotypes in these shows are normalized they are more easily accepted.

According to Hinton (2000), stereotypes are a persuasive view of the world, they can be right or wrong, and they are linked to our understanding of why people are who they are. Hinton argues that stereotyping involves judging people in a typical category as members rather than individuals. He says there are four key ideas in the debates surrounding stereotyping.

> First, we have the view that stereotypes arise from the limitation of human cognitive processes: perception and knowledge are arrived at through the process of constructing simplified pictures of the world. Second, the contents of stereotypes are provided by the culture of the person. Third, both the stereotyping process and the contents of the stereotype are faulty because the resultant stereotype is almost certainly an inaccurate picture of the real world. Finally, the negative connotation of stereotyping and stereotypes (that is they are not good things) is further supported by the belief that they are not flexible and therefore not easy to change. (p. 9)

Balancing Stereotypes

Olivia Pope appeared amidst a loud flurry of positive headlines: "With *Scandal* New Visibility for Black Women on TV" (Deggans, 2012), "*Scandal* on *ABC* is Breaking Barriers" (Black Voices, 2013), "In Creating *Scandal* and Olivia Pope, Shonda Rhimes Changed the TV Landscape" (Obell, 2018), and "Kerry Washington Effect: How TV Ditched Stereotypes to make History" (Strauss, 2014). A historic fact, Olivia Pope was the first black female lead in a prime-time show since *Get Christie Love* in 1974 (IMDb).

Olivia's character defied traditional black female stereotypes as an impressive black female gladiator. She was intelligent and powerful, even though that intelligence and power was sometimes used illegally and immorally. She was a well-known fixer among the Washington, DC political realm which meant her company stepped in to help with problems. Olivia's strength was demonstrated in her skills for negotiation, crisis management, and problem solving (Perkins, 2013).

Unfortunately, the Jezebel stereotype was also a core part of Pope's character. She was sexually aggressive and impetuous as her affair with the married president of the United States of America confirmed. When she was not sleeping with President Fitzgerald Grant III, Pope would land in the arms of Navy Intelligence Officer Jake Ballard. And in between those relationships the audience learns about her previous fiancé a U.S. Congressman and a one-night stand with a Latino reporter.

Olivia also displayed several mammy characteristics such as the need to take care of everyone. Despite the fact that her thin body, expensive clothes, and well-manicured hands are nothing like a traditional mammy, Olivia was depicted as a caregiver. Maxwell (2013) argues that Olivia served the massah's house, The White House and made sure it functioned the way it should just like the traditional mammy during slavery. Maxwell also discussed Olivia's dip into the angry black woman or Sapphire stereotype every now and then. For example, a confrontation between President Mellie Grant and Olivia in the Oval Office shows her taking charge.

> Olivia "There's three things you need to know about me that you should already know but I clearly need to reiterate. One, you do not ignore me, because two, I'm right always. It's frustrating get used to it. And three there is only us, you and me. That's all there is. We have it all. The people, the pulpit, the purse strings, guns, all of it, everything is ours to deploy for the betterment and defense of the people and office we serve. The men outside these oval walls they want to take it all away from us because they are terrified, they are outraged because they have come to the realization that all of those years of misogyny and privilege and status quo are finally over. That is why you never listen to a man over me. Your success as president is my only agenda. I alone have your back always. You want to keep the barbarians at the gate? You want to hold these walls? You want to keep having it all? Reverse the tides of injustice, redraw the map, flood the darkness with light, earn our place and make it so that a woman in this office is no longer a novelty but the norm, then you have to stop thinking of me as an employee and start thinking of me as what I am. Mellie "And what is that?" Olivia "The boss. Put your faith in me and me alone and you will become a monument. Ignore me, allow them to come between us and you will become an asterisk." (Philippe, 2018)

Annalise Keating is a prominent lawyer and professor teaching at a private university on the east coast. She runs a law firm out of her home with student interns. Annalise's character is defined by the title of the show, *How to get Away with Murder*. She is not a lawyer who always follows the rules. Her goal is to win no matter what and that is what she teaches her students.

A major debate evolved when *New York Times* television critic Stanley (2014) wrote that based on Shonda Rhimes characters, her autobiography should be titled "How to get away with being an angry black woman" (D'addario, 2014; Giorgis, 2014; Nordyke, 2014). Brown (2014) explains why that angry black woman stereotype is a problematic racial trope.

> Black women aren't allowed to be complicated—they're just angry. Black women aren't allowed to be upset or vulnerable—they're just angry. Black women are not allowed justifiable reactions to the myriad of bullshit—racist, sexist and otherwise—that they face. (Brown, 2014)

Unfortunately, because of that stereotype it is hard for black women characters to show real emotion. Stanley (2014) goes on to compare Annalise to Claire Huxtable's character. She says that "Claire is serene, elegant, and reassuring while Annalise is sexual and even sexy in a slightly menacing way ... older, darker skinned and less classically beautiful than Ms. Washington or for that matter Halle Berry." The comparison of Viola Davis to Kerry Washington or Halle Berry suggests that an older, more domineering woman who is not seen as the white standard of beauty presents a problem.

Annalise's character is one that demands respect. She has a take charge and stay in control personality. Her role as a black woman offers depth and intricacy, despite the stereotypes that surface. She is married to her former therapist in the pilot, but having an affair with a Philadelphia detective Nate Lahey. Nate is married as well, but his wife is ill. Annalise also serves as a mammy archetype concerning her student interns. Not in the way she dresses or talks, of course, but in a more general sense as the strong caretaker and defender, along with her darker color of her skin. In contrast, she is a professional, upper-class attorney who demonstrates an alternative to the typical media stereotypes of jezebels, mammies, and angry black women.

Attorney Toms-Anthony (2018) registers concern with the professional stereotypes that are perpetuated in shows like *How to get Away with Murder*. He worries that they could lead to implicit bias concerning black female attorneys in reality. According to Toms-Anthony, the mammy stereotype can be attached to Annalise based on characteristics like loyalty, faithfulness, all knowing, and all understanding. The modern-day jezebel stereotype also suggests that black women are sexually aggressive with Annalise playing a tempting seductress when it comes to Nate and Emmett. Finally, he argues that Annalise is also shown throughout the series as an aggressive, angry black woman in the classroom, in her personal life, and as an attorney in the courtroom.

Dr. Miranda Bailey in *Grey's Anatomy* has worked her way up from chief resident to Chief of Surgery at Seattle Grace Hospital. Her nickname is "the NAZI." In the pilot, Miranda is shown as the stereotypical angry black woman telling her interns that her rules are the law, so don't bother sucking up because she already hates them and that's not going to change (Mathis, 2017). However, she also falls into the mammy stereotype offering tough and unconditional love. Her life is focused on her interns and she will protect them no matter what. In one episode, Miranda actually orders her grown interns to take a time out just like she would a child. Also, like the mammy caricature, Miranda's own child is not as important in her life as her interns, we rarely see her son, while her co-worker Meredith's kids are featured in a number of episodes.

After a failed marriage leaves Miranda as a single parent, she remarries Ben Warren and is shown in a normal relationship for a while which is rare for black women on television. As a doctor Miranda's role on *Grey's Anatomy* gives us a solid picture of how a black woman can achieve excellence. She is a great surgeon, a compassionate doctor, and she can stand her ground with any of the other doctors at Seattle Grace when it comes to intelligence.

Godin (2014) disagrees with the label of angry black women for Rhimes's characters, "*Scandal's* Olivia Pope, *Grey's Anatomy's* Dr. Bailey, and *Murder's* Annalise Keating aren't angry black women. While they get angry at some points, just like any television character does, that's not the emotion that defines them."

The stereotypes for black men on television are many, but the most prominent are negative images related to the criminal justice system. Smiley and Fakunle (2016) write that the early historical stereotype of the black brute has been replaced by the contemporary black thug. In their study, they connect the use of deadly force used in real life by police on unarmed black men to this prevalent biased frame of black men as criminals.

Media research in the 1990s found that news stories about crime most likely focused on black, violent crime. It was more often associated with black suspects and black suspects were usually shown as threatening or dangerous (Entman, 1992). Early reality based crime shows depicted approximately 62% of police officers as white and 77% of suspects as black and Latino (Oliver, 1994). Page (1997), called early black media imagery "unembraceable." She argues that only a few black men mainly celebrities, athletes, musicians, and politicians were given positive status in the media.

According to Wheeling (2015) most people learn about the criminal justice system by watching films and television shows. She added that fictional images does influence how people understand police conduct and legal issues. In a content analysis from the 2001 season of two crime dramas *Law and Order* and *NYPD Blue*, Eschholz, Mallard, and Flynn (2004) found that black characters were more likely to be shown as offenders rather than victims of crime. They worried that such images were reinforcing the perception that people of color, especially blacks pose a serious social threat to society.

The consistent stereotypes of black males as criminals, thugs, gangbangers, drug dealers, and overall villains is difficult to remove. Yet, there is a more balanced image emerging on prime-time television. Strong, powerful black men within the criminal justice system are not depicted as stereotypes but instead as captains, detectives, sergeants, and chiefs. These important and commanding images display an essential alternative to the negative norms.

L L Cool J plays Sam Hanna a former Navy Seal now working as a Senior Field Agent at *NCIS*. Sam is fluent in Arabic and five other languages including Spanish, Korean, and Hebrew (Seitz, 2011). He is a loyal and thoughtful partner helping whenever he can to support and encourage the team. Sam likes to build things. In season one he talks about how important it is for a man to be able to create with his hands. One hobby he shows off is his work with origami. In different episodes we also discover that he does not like maggots (Season 1) and he has a fear of clowns (Season 4) too.

In the season nine opener (Arbonida, 2017), Sam spends his first holiday with his kids after his wife has been killed. He met his wife during a joint mission with the CIA to stop a Russian Arms dealer. Later his wife was kidnapped and killed by a terrorist out to get Sam. Of course, Sam seeks revenge for his wife's murder and succeeds. Sam as a family man was an important element for balance. Sadly, losing his wife meant a loss of that sense of normalcy for Sam and his two kids.

Sergeant Odafin Tutuola is a former Army Ranger. This character has been played by former rapper, Ice T for almost 20 years on *Law and Order Special Victims Unit* (1999). Tutuola serves as a balancing image for black criminal stereotypes on his show and throughout the media in general. In one episode, Tutuola's son, Ken, by his ex-wife learns that he has a half-brother, Darious. Darious is responsible for a murder, but he is acquitted of the charge despite his guilt. Both Ken and Tutuola decide the right thing to do is to stay out of it and keep their distance.

Tutuola is a street-smart character on *Law and Order SVU*. In an interview with *TV Insider*, Ice T admits that in his past life as a rapper he was resistant to the police (Rudolph, 2019). However, after playing this role, he says he now understands that they work hard and are underpaid. Ice T added that he has also seen the blue wall that exists between officers where the police will support and cover for each other (Rudolph, 2019). In various episodes, he confronts his captain about not allocating the same level of manpower to a serial killer of black woman as white women, he discovers a slavery ring among the rich telling one of the leaders "In case you haven't heard Lincoln freed the slaves," and it takes him a while but eventually he accepts the fact that his son is gay.

Shemar Moore moved to *SWAT* as Daniel Hondo Harrelson after spending 11 seasons as Derick Morgan on *Criminal Minds* where he won a People's Choice Award. Moore also earned 8 NAACP Image Awards on *Criminal Minds* (Carter, 2017). His new show, Hondo tackles controversial issues like bad cops policing black communities, Black Lives Matter protests, Trump's perpetuation of racism, fear, and distrust, plus the injustice and conflict that black people face daily.

The 1992 Los Angeles riots were fueled by issues of systematic discrimination and racial profiling within the Los Angeles Special Weapons and Tactics division (Carr, 2018). The plot of *SWAT* was designed to address the conflict between the police and black communities after the riots. As Carr explains Hondo's character struggles to bridge the gap because he has a past that included gang activity. When his friend Leroy contacts Hondo from jail and asks him to help his son Daryl who is in trouble Hondo agrees. Hondo was able to escape the gang life, so going back into the old neighborhood to help Daryl is a serious endeavor (Vick, 2017). In season two, Daryl witnesses a drive-by shooting and he is stabbed in detention. Hondo helps to get him out and keep him safe. Taking this young brother under his wing is a noteworthy example of balance for black male characters on television. Daryl's father didn't make it out of the vicious cycle of violence and prison, but with Hondo's help maybe Daryl can take a different path.

Morris Chestnut as Will Keaton an FBI agent on *The Enemy Within* is introduced with a hard edge. His fiancé was killed by a terrorist and he is working with the traitor who gave the terrorist his fiancé's name (Grove, 2019). Unlike the stereotypical young black thug who wears baggy pants and hoodies, Will is professionally styled in tailored suits and ties, sporting a smooth, bald head, and a tightly shaped mustache with goatee. Although, his character seems stern, he does have a heart. He shows it as he struggles to help the traitor who was forced to make a choice to save her own daughter by giving up the names of the agents who were killed.

A balanced representation of black women and men in prime-time television is relevant to the issue of racialism. There is, of course, a long way to go in order to achieve equality, but this is a good start. It is movement toward the changing the traditional stereotypes in black culture that are normalized in mainstream media. Some may argue that it is difficult to change black male and female stereotypes, but not impossible? The prominence of complex and oppositional images illustrates that black characters can be more than stereotypes. As we watch more complicated human beings on the small scree the essentialist notion of black equals ghetto might eventually be eliminated.

Gray (2005) writes that television programs about crime and the law are used as a means to establish normative legitimacy and moral propriety.

> In matters of race and representation, law and legal discourse are especially crucial because they are the structuring scenes or sites in which organizing narratives about fairness, civility, propriety, transgression, and responsibility are framed. (p. 22)

As the popularity of alternative images continue to emerge through the balancing of stereotypical black male and female roles hopefully it will make a difference someday in the way society perceives black cultural reality.

References

Arbonida, J. (2017, December 14). *NCIS Los Angeles* Season 9 Episode 11. *The Christian Post*. Retrieved from https://www.christianpost.com/trends/ncis-los-angeles-season-9-episode-11-spoilers-sam-celebrates-first-holidays-without-wife.html

Black Voices. (2013, January 17). *Scandal* on *ABC* is Breaking Barriers (*New York Times*). *Huffpost*. Retrieved from https://www.huffingtonpost.com/entry/scandal-on-abc-is-breaking-barriers_n_2499491.html

Bogle, D. (2016). *Toms, Coons, Mulattoes, Mammies, and Bucks: An interpretive history of Blacks in American films* (4th ed.). New York, NY: Bloomsbury Academic.

Brown, K. (2014, September 19). *The New York Times*, Shonda Rhimes and how to get away with being a racist. *Jezebel*. Retrieved from https://jezebel.com/the-new-york-times-shonda-rhimes-how-to-get-away-wit-1636868442

Brown-Givens, S., & Monahan, J. (2005, February 1). Priming mammies, jezebels, and other controlling images: An examination of the influence of mediated stereotypes on perceptions of African American women. *Media Psychology, 7*(1), 87–106.

Carr, F. (2018, July 6). We're bridging the gap between civilians and cops: *S.W.A.T.* is a fun, action-packed drama with hidden depths. *RadioTimes*. Retrieved from https://www.radiotimes.com/news/tv/2018-07-06/swat-shemar-moore-sky-one-police-drama-black-lives-matter/

Carr, T. (October 12, 2014). Why are all of the powerful black women on TV sleeping with married men? *Examiner.com*. Retrieved from http://www.examiner.com/article/why-are-all-of-the-powerful-black-women-on-tv-promiscuous

Carter, K. (2017, November 2). Shemar Moore takes a Leap of Faith from *Criminal Minds* to *SWAT*. *The Undefeated*. Retrieve from https://theundefeated.com/features/producer-actor-shemar-moore-swat-criminal-minds-cbs/

Cops. (1989–). IMDb. Retrieved from https://www.imdb.com/title/tt0096563/

D'addario, D. (2014, September 23). Alessandra Stanley's pathetic non-apology for her Shonda Rhimes "Angry Black Woman" review. *Salon.* Retrieved from https://www.salon.com/2014/09/22/alessandra_stanleys_pathetic_non_apology_for_her_shonda_rhimes_angry black_woman_review/

Deggans, E. (2012, April 5). With *Scandal* new visibility for black women on TV. *NPR.* Retrieved from https://www.npr.org/2012/04/05/149998991/with-scandal-abc-targets-black-female-viewers

The Enemy Within. (2019–). IMDb. Retrieved from: https://www.imdb.com/title/tt8390342/

Entman, R. (1992). Blacks in news: Television, modern racism and social change. *Journalism and Mass Communication Quarterly, 69*(2), 341–361.

Entman, R., & Rojecki, A. (2001). *The black image in the white mind: Media and race in America.* Chicago, IL: University of Chicago Press.

Eschholz, S., Mallard, M., & Flynn, S. (2004). Images of prime-time justice: A content analysis of NYPD Blue and Law and Order. *Journal of Criminal Justice and Popular Culture, 10*(3), 161–180.

Gerbner, G., Gross, L., Morgan, M., & Signorielle, N. (2002). Growing up with television: The cultivation perspective. In J. Bryant & D. Zillman (Eds.), *Media effects: Advances in theory and research.* Hillsdale, NJ: Lawrence Erlbaum.

Get Christie Love. (1974). IMDb. Retrieved from https://www.imdb.com/title/tt0070990/

Giorgis, H. (2014, September 22). The myth of the angry black woman is a scandal of white supremacy. *The Guardian.* Retrieved from https://www.theguardian.com/commentisfree/2014/sep/22/angry-black-woman-new-york-times-shonda-rhimes

Godin, J. (2014, September 21). Shonda Rhimes slams *New York Times* for angry black woman label. *AJC.* Retrieved from https://www.ajc.com/entertainment/shonda-rhimes-slams-new-york-times-for-angry-black-woman-label/vzTHMsiWYzqHmuqpzCnAMI/

Gray, H. (2005). *Cultural moves: African Americans and the politics of representation.* Oakland: University of California Press.

Grey's Anatomy. (2005–). Retrieved from https://www.imdb.com/title/tt0413573/

Grove, R. (2019, February 25). Morris Chestnut to Star in New NBC Series pilot *The Enemy Within. The Source.* Retrieved from http://thesource.com/2019/02/25/morris-chestnut-to-star-in-new-nbc-series-pilot-the-enemy-within/

Harris-Perry, M. (2011). *Sister citizen shame: Stereotypes and black women in America.* New Haven: Yale University Press.

Hinton, P. (2000). *Stereotypes, cognition and culture.* New York, NY: Routledge

How to Get Away with Murder. (2014–). IMDb. Retrieved from https://www.imdb.com/title/tt3205802/

Jewell, S. K. (1993). *From mammy to Miss America and beyond: Cultural images and the shaping of U.S. policy.* New York, NY: Routledge.

Kay, A. (2015, January 14). Is *Empire* a *Hustle and Flow* sequel? Because that sounds pretty fantastic. *Bustle.com.* Retrieved from http://www.bustle.com/articles/58491-is-empire-a-hustle-flow-sequel-because-that-sounds-pretty-fantastic

Koblin, J. (2018, July 20). Shonda Rhimes describes her grand Netflix ambitions. *The New York Times*. Retrieved from https://www.nytimes.com/2018/07/20/business/media/shonda-rhimes-netflix-series.html

Krantz-Kent, R. (2018, September). Television capturing America's attention prime-time and beyond. *Bureau of Labor Statistics*. Retrieved from https://www.bls.gov/opub/btn/volume-7/television-capturing-americas-attention.htm

Law and Order: SVU. (1999–). IMDb. Retrieved from https://www.imdb.com/title/tt0203259/

Mastro, D. (2017, September 26). Race and ethnicity in U.S. media contents and effects. *Oxford Research Encyclopedias*. New York, NY: Oxford University Press.

Mastro, D., & Greenberg, B. (2000). The portrayal of racial minorities on prime-time television. *Journal of Broadcasting and Electronic Media*, *44*(4), 690–703.

Mathis, C. (2017). *Mammy-tracking Bailey: The intersection of race and motherhood in Grey's anatomy*. Murfreesboro, TN: Middle Tennessee State University/Academia.

Maxwell, B. (2013, March 26). Olivia Pope and the scandal of representation. *SCN*. Retrieved from http://sparechangenews.net/2013/03/olivia-pope-the-scandal-of-representation/

Monk-Turner, E., Heiserman, M., Johnson, C., Cotton, V., & Jackson M. (2010, Spring). The portrayal of racial minorities on prime-time television: A replication of the Mastro and Greenberg study a decade later. *Studies in Popular Culture*, *32*(2), 101–114.

NCIS Los Angeles. (2009–). IMDb. Retrieved from: https://www.imdb.com/title/tt1378167/

Neilson Insights. (2017, February 8). For us by us? The mainstream appeal of black content. *Neilson.com* Retrieved from https://www.nielsen.com/us/en/insights/news/2017/for-us-by-us-the-mainstream-appeal-of-black-content.html

New York Undercover. (1994–1999). IMDb. Retrieved from https://www.imdb.com/title/tt0108876/

Nordyke, K. (2014, September 22). NYT public editor: Article about Shonda Rhimes was "astonishingly tone-deaf," "out of touch". *Hollywood Reporter*. Retrieved from https://www.hollywoodreporter.com/news/shonda-rhimes-angry-black-woman-734658

NYPD Blue. (1993–2005). IMDb. Retrieved from https://www.imdb.com/title/tt0106079/

Obell, S. (2018, April 19). In creating *Scandal* and Olivia Pope, Shonda Rhimes changed the TV landscape. *Buzzfeed*. Retrieved from https://www.buzzfeednews.com/article/sylviaobell/scandal-series-finale-legacy

Oliver, M. B. (1994). Portrayals of crime, race and aggression in "reality based" police shows: a content analysis. *Journal of Broadcasting and Electronic Media*, 38(2), 179–192.

Page, H. (1997). Black imagery and media containment of African American men. *American Anthropologist*, *99*(1), 99–111.

Perkins, N. (2013, October 24). It's time to say goodbye to TVs strong black women. *BuzzFeed*. Retrieved from https://www.buzzfeed.com/tnwhiskeywoman/scandal-sleepy-hollow-destroy-strong-black-woman-stereotype

Philippe, B. (2018, April 17). Olivia Pope isn't a hero and that's been *Scandal's* point all along. *Vanity Fair*. Retrieved from https://www.vanityfair.com/hollywood/2018/04/scandal-series-finale-olivia-pope-kerry-washington-antihero-shonda-rhimes

Plous, S & Williams, T. (1995, May). Racial stereotypes from the days of American slavery: A continuing legacy. *Journal of Applied Social Psychology, 25*(9), 795–817.

Private Practice. (2007–2013). IMDB. Retrieved from https://www.imdb.com/title/tt0972412/

Punyanunt-Carter, N. M. (2008). The Perceived Realism of African American Portrayal on Television. *Howard Journal of Communications, 19*(3), 241–257.

Ripley, K. (2017, February 16). 15 Epic One-Liners that prove that Ice-T makes *Law and Order: SVU*. *TheThings.com* Retrieved from https://www.thethings.com/15-epic-one-liners-that-prove-that-ice-t-makes-law-and-order-svu/

Rudolph, I. (2019, February 14). *Law and Order: SVU*: Ice T sounds off on romance for Tutuola and his complicated feelings on cops. *TV Insider*. Retrieved from https://www.tvinsider.com/752430/ice-t-law-order-svu-fin-tutuola-phoebe-baker-jennifer-esposito/

Scandal. (2012–2018). Retrieved from https://www.imdb.com/title/tt1837576/

Seitz, M. (2011, March 22). The underappreciated excellence of LL Cool J. *Salon*. Retrieved from https://www.salon.com/2011/03/22/ll_cool_j_ncis/

Shonda Rhimes makes TV that represents everyone. (2018, October 10). *Elle Magazine*. Retrieved from https://www.elle.com/culture/movies-tv/a23689555/shonda-rhimes-shondaland-netflix/

Smiley, C. J., & Fakunle, D. (2016). From brute to thug: The demonization and criminalization of unarmed black male victims in America. *Journal of Human Behavior and Social Environment, 26*(3–4), 350–366.

Stanley, A. (2014, September 18). Wrought in Rhimes's image. *The New York Times*. Retrieved from https://www.nytimes.com/2014/09/21/arts/television/viola-davis-plays-shonda-rhimess-latest-tough-heroine.html

Station 19. (2018–). IMDb. Retrieved from https://www.imdb.com/title/tt7053188/

Strauss, J. (2014, May 15). Kerry Washington effect: How TV ditched stereotypes to make history. *NBC News*. Retrieved from https://www.nbcnews.com/pop-culture/tv/kerry-washington-effect-how-tv-ditched-stereotypes-make-history-n106886

SWAT. (2017–). IMDb. Retrieved from https://www.imdb.com/title/tt6111130/

Toll, R. (1974). *Blacking up: The minstrel show in nineteenth-century America*. New York, NY: Oxford University Press.

Toms-Anthony, S. (2018). Annalise Keating's portrayal as an attorney is the real scandal: Examining how the use of stereotypical depictions of black women can lead to the formation of implicit biases. *National Black Law Journal, 27*(1), 59–78.

Turner, P. (2002). *Ceramic uncles & celluloid mammies: Black images and their influence on culture*. Charlottesville, VA: University of Virginia Press.

Umstead, R. T. (2018, August 23). Horowitz: Nearly three quarters of African American viewers stream TV content. *Multichannel News*. Retrieved from https://www.multichannel.com/blog/horowitz-nearly-three-quarters-of-african-american-viewers-stream-tv-content

VanderWerff, T. (2018, April 20). 5 ways Scandal changed television forever. Vox. Retrieved from https://www.vox.com/culture/2018/4/19/17259142/scandal-series-finale-review-recap-impact

Vick, M. (2017, December 13). S.W.A.T. Exclusive: Hondo has to revisit his Gang Past. *TV Guide* Retrieved from https://www.tvguide.com/news/swat-exclusive-hondo-gang-past/

Vrij, A., Van Schie, E & Cherryman, J. (1996). Reducing ethnic prejudice through public communication programs. *Journal of Psychology, 4*, 413–420.

Weigel, R., Kim, E & Frost, J. (1995). Race relations of prime-time television reconsidered: Patterns of continuity and change. *Journal of Applied Social Psychology, 25*, 223–236.

Wheeling, K. (2015, October 1). How prime-time TV influences perceptions of police. *Pacific Standard*. Retrieved from https://psmag.com/social-justice/law-and-order-is-educational-television

Witter, B. (2018, December 26). Dr. Miranda Bailey's 11 best Grey's Anatomy' one-liners will take you down memory lane. *Bustle*. Retrieved from https://www.bustle.com/p/dr-miranda-baileys-11-best-greys-anatomy-one-liners-will-take-you-down-memory-lane-15566719

CHAPTER SIX

A Satirical Parody: Black Jesus in the Hood

According to the Pew Research Center (Masci, 2018; Diamant, 2018), approximately 79% of African Americans self-identify as Christian, African Americans are more religious than whites and LatinX, plus African Americans are more likely to read the Bible regularly and believe that it represents God's word. Religion is a critical component of the black community and many scholars argue that the description of Jesus in the Bible where his hair is like wool and feet the color of fine brass means he was not white (Cone, 2010). Cone actually believes that not only was Jesus black based on his description in the Bible, but symbolically since Jesus bonded with the oppressed, the poor, and the downtrodden, it more likely that he was a person of color.

So, what happened when Aaron McGruder and Mike Clattenburg created an *Adult Swim* parody called *Black Jesus*? The American Family Association came out against the show immediately based on its trailer (De Moraes, 2014). According to *Deadline Hollywood* the group was concerned that the show was blasphemous and made a mockery of Jesus Christ. One Million Moms (2018) were upset when the show returned for a second season calling it a sacrilegious program that distorts the truth about Christianity. Several black preachers also expressed concern such as Kerry Burkey, senior pastor at the Rockledge Church of Christ in Florida who said the show confirms that our nation has no respect for God (Gallop, 2014).

The controversial production also had a number of supporters. *CNN's* Don Lemon said on the *Tom Joiner Show* that *Black Jesus* is a way of educating people through humor.

> Have we really become so polarized and so sensitive that we have lost our sense of humor? Now ask yourself, what would Jesus do? I think he'd probably at least watch the first episode before jumping to conclusions and let he who is without sin or in this case without a sense of humor cast the first stone. (Feldman, 2014)

Pastor Leslie Callahan of St. Paul's Baptist Church in Philadelphia wrote in *Time Magazine* (2014) that depicting Jesus as a money-hungry capitalist like some of the current mega churches do is just as blasphemous as showing him cursing and smoking pot in the hood. She also suggested that people should be as worried about the limitation of women's roles in certain churches and religious denominations as they are about a fictional television show.

The co-creator of *Black Jesus* Aaron McGruder is no stranger to controversy. His earlier animated show *Boondocks* was a satirical look at blacks moving out to the suburbs. It included lots of stereotypes upsetting members of the black community on many occasions. McGruder defended his new show saying, "Black Jesus comes in peace offering morality lessons and questioning the state of modern society" (Braxton, 2014).

In the show, Black Jesus, the Son of God lives in the hood (Compton). He hangs with his crew (or as he calls them his disciples). He wears sandals, a dingy white gown covered by a brown robe and his long, relaxed hair falls down past his shoulders. This Black Jesus not only spouts bible verses, but he curses, calls God "Pops," and smokes weed.

It is easy, based on the description above, to talk about how this representation of Black Jesus perpetuates negative stereotypes, but the show also does something more interesting. It questions religion, the Bible, and God's word in relation to the experience of living in poverty in America in the twenty-first century. In this chapter, I explore how racialism is used to examine the hypocrisy of society's religious ideology and behavior when it comes stereotypes of poor and black people in America's inner cities.

Stereotypes and Satire

There has been significant research that examines race, media and stereotypes. Some examples include, racial stereotypes on realty shows (Tyree, 2011); stereotyping black male athletes (Hodge, Burden, Robinson, & Bennett, 2008); children's stereotypes in advertising (Gilmore & Jordan, 2012); stereotypes of mammies and matriarchs (Sewell, 2013); black criminal stereotypes (Welch, 2007); black media stereotypes and racial identity (Adams-Bass, Stevenson, & Kotzin, 2014); reinforcing stereotypes in Congress through TV news coverage (Schaffner & Gadson, 2004); and perceptions surrounding stereotypes of fictional characters (Sanders & Ramasubramanian, 2012).

Bryson and Davis (2010) are concerned that stereotypes produce boundaries. They discuss four theoretical limitations integral to the use of stereotypes. First, social structure is often absolved by stereotypes. Inequality is blamed on individual bias and the systematic process is not confronted. Second, usually stereotypes move in one direction influencing social and symbolic boundaries. Third, people participate in their own oppression through stereotypes. In other words, each side accepts and promotes their own boundaries. Fourth, stereotyping preserves the distinction between groups, so even when sharing the same space people remain racially and ethnically separated.

In her research on "double distinction," Epstein (1992, 2010) examines how physical and conceptual differences between various groups actually can create boundaries. And Douglas (2002), offers an example in the clash between religion and inner-city stereotypes observing how such boundaries can explain a host of behaviors aimed at preserving various differences in the face of conflicting categories of meaning.

Parody and satire usually include stereotypes. Stereotypical humor is often used as a satirical and parodic tool to critique specific situations. Researchers have found that satire and parody are eminent in times of crisis. According to McClennen and Maisel (2014) satire is more than entertainment because it allows important political discourse to reach a broad number of people. For example, McClennen (2019) believes late night comedy satire can have a huge impact on the 2020 election. He argues that hosts like Trevor Noah of *The Daily Show*, Samantha Bee on *Full Frontal*, Stephen Cobert on *The Late Show*, Jimmy Fallon's *Tonight Show*, *Late Night* with Seth Meyers and even *Saturday Night Live* will continue to influence the news, inform viewers, frame debates, and shape public opinion.

McClennen and Maisel (2014) worry that too many people don't understand the larger purpose of satire or parody. Many dismiss it as just entertainment or attack it as mockery and ridicule. In a discussion about satire in the post-civil rights era, Beckson and Ganz (1989) define satire as a subject being ridiculed to point out its faults. However, parody is also seen as an imitation of something in order to criticize it by Holman and Harmon (1992). Finally, satire and parody both use elements of sarcasm, irony and humor to construct and deconstruct meaning

(Kreuz & Roberts, 1993). Dickson-Carr (2001) see parody and satire as significant to the politics of conversion.

> The greatest possibilities are that African American satirists will continue to draw upon black vernacular discourse and cultural tradition since they have served black literature so well and offer rich counter-points to the vagaries of mainstream American culture by shedding light on what satire means to African Americans. The meaning has numerous permutations but the central stake is the continued existence of African Americans. (p. 207)

Gray (2005) insists that contemporary black cultural programs that use parody, humor, irony, shock, irreverence, transgression, and spectacle must have audience investment.

> The payoff is worth the investment because if nothing else, irony and parody help to illuminate the precarious nature of representation (especially racial stereotypes). Politically, the gain is that representations deploying these strategies reveal the degree to which cultural meaning and relations organized through social power are anchored and produced in history (and not in nature). (p. 128)

These tactics have been used effectively to critique mainstream American culture particularly through black sitcoms and other media venues. Since satire and parody are based on the absurd they have the ability to get people to think outside of the norm. In other words, any analysis of parodic portrayals in relation to black culture must take into account the need for such extremity in humor.

Jesus in the Bible

Some people will argue that the description of Jesus in *the Bible* more closely resembles a person of color than not. In Revelation (1:15) it reads, "his feet were like burnished bronze, refined in a furnace." In Revelation (1:14) it also reads, "the hairs on his head were white, like white wool." According to Wayne (2017), author of *Jesus is Black, Get Over It*, science suggests geographically and genetically that Jesus had brown skin. King Solomon's wife was black, so black people existed during that period and research has shown that there were Africans living among the Israelites from countries like Egypt and Ethiopia. Adams (2018) explains that the prophet Jeremiah mentions Africa and Africans more than 100 times in the Old Testament. As a matter of fact, Ethiopians, Cushites and Kedarians had dark complexions. In chapter 13, verse 23 Jeremiah asks, "Can an Ethiopian change his skin or a leopard its spots?" In the Song of Solomon (1:5) a Shulammite woman speaks to the king's court, "Dark am I, yet lovely, daughters of Jerusalem, dark like the tents of Kedar, like the tent curtains of Solomon" (Hays, 2003).

Jesus spent his life spreading the word of God among the people of God. He lived with the poor, the ill, and the oppressed. Jesus tells us that we will always have the poor with us and that we have a duty to help them. "Verily I say unto you, inasmuch as ye have done it unto one of the least of these my brethren, ye have done it unto me" (Matthew 25:40).

> The Spirit of the Lord is upon me, because he hath anointed me to preach the gospel to the poor; he hath sent me to heal the broken hearted; to preach deliverance to the captives, and recovering of sight to the blind, to set at liberty them that are bruised, to preach the acceptable year of the Lord. (Luke 4:18–19)

Jesus' disciples also accepted a life with sinners and the poor when they worked on his behalf. *The Bible* talks about how certain groups were treated very poorly. For example, the Samaritans were harassed and looked down on by others. In the story of the "Good Samaritan" it is important to understand how Jesus related to this negated group of people. It was Luke 10 where Jesus is asked by a lawyer how to gain eternal life and Jesus tells him to follow the law, "Thou shalt love the Lord thy God with all thy heart, and with all thy soul, and with all thy strength, and with all they mind; and love thy neighbor as thyself."

Jesus goes on to tell the lawyer the story of a man who came down from Jerusalem to Jericho, and fell among thieves from Luke 10:25–37. They stripped him of his supplies, wounded him, and departed, leaving him half dead. A priest came down that way, but when he saw the man he passed by on the other side. And likewise, a Levite, passed too after looking at him. But a good Samaritan, as he journeyed saw the man and had compassion on him. He bound up the man's wounds, set him on his own beast, and brought him to an inn paying them to take care of him.

Another story from the Sermon on the Mount explains that the first words spoken by the Lord were: "Blessed are the poor in spirit: for theirs is the kingdom of heaven" (Matthew 5:3). When Lazarus, a slave, dies begging the rich man for food he is carried by the angels into heaven. Later, when that rich man dies he is sent to hell, but still thinks he has power, so he asks the Lord to send him water through his slave Lazarus. The Lord tells the rich man that things have changed. Lazarus will be comforted while the rich man will exist in torment.

Even in the story of the woman with the issue of blood we learn that we should have compassion for those who are sick or in trouble (Luke, 8). The woman had spent all of her money trying to find a cure for her illness with no success. Too often people think they are better than others. This woman was considered unclean and anyone who touched her was labeled the same way. After suffering for twelve years she was desperate, so she followed Jesus until she was able to touch the hem of his garment. She prayed to be healed and her prayers were answered. Jesus stopped walking and pointed her out because he wanted everyone to see what God had done for this woman based on her strong faith.

Black Jesus

Many of these principles of the Bible are involved as Black Jesus serves the people of Compton, California. However, there is an obvious tension between Black Jesus and some residents. Gerald "Slink" Johnson at six foot five is a demanding presence (Loury, 2014). In Season 1/Episode 1, we are introduced to Black Jesus as he walks down the street and stops to talk to a homeless man. The homeless man, Lloyd, jumps up from his old chair on the street and hugs Jesus tightly.

Lloyd:	"Alright Jesus what chu got for me today, I been good?"
Black Jesus:	"Talk good to me brotha, the world is yours, whatever you want."
Lloyd (rubs his hands together):	"I need the numbers to the Lotto."
Black Jesus:	"The Lotto numbers? Is that the best you can ask man? I mean, there's folks out here dying of famine and pestilence and you want the Lotto numbers. Come on man you can do better than that."
Lloyd:	"What can you give me then?"
Black Jesus:	"I got some kindness, I got compassion and I got love for all mankind. You better get up on some of that man."
Lloyd (frowns):	"Don't nobody want no shit like that!"

The conversation goes downhill from there as they begin to play the dozens. Black Jesus tells Lloyd he stinks and Lloyd says Black Jesus looks like Obi-Wan Kenobi in his brown robe. Next, Black Jesus describes Lloyd's hair as full of Brillo pads, Lloyd gets mad, and stomps away. Black Jesus calls after him, "I still love your bitch-ass by default fool."

This jarring representation of a Black Jesus that curses and plays the dozens is parody tied to a satirical racial consciousness. We see Black Jesus with long straight brown hair, while Lloyd's hair is compared to Brillo pads, a closer substance to the wool described on Jesus's head in *The Bible*. The show offers a powerful vision of stereotypical images and ideas in urban black culture met with the resistance of a contemporary version of God's word. Lloyd wants to win the Lotto, that is his savior in the twenty-first century not God. When Black Jesus steers him away from the societal notion of capitalism and greed the conversation blows up.

A critical analysis reveals layers of religious and cultural meaning throughout the various episodes in this show. There is a purposeful clash between religion's moral superiority and how the poor, stressed urban population is forced to live. Black Jesus offers a complicated message to the oppressed. He represents both an insider and an outsider in the black community.

Later in the first episode, Black Jesus and his crew (the disciples) are smoking a joint. When Black Jesus holds on to the joint too long, the group complains that he is always smoking up all the weed and he doesn't pay for any it. Black Jesus gets annoyed and tells them that their complaints are trivial.

Black Jesus:	"You really fixen to get at me like that over some funky-ass weed? You do realize that I died for your M'F' sins right?"
Jason:	"Oh, that shit's gettin' old."
Black Jesus:	"Homey that's my life!"

When Black Jesus suggests that they start a community garden to grow their own weed, plus vegetables one of the crew (Fish) jokes that he doesn't want to be a farmer. Black Jesus is constantly pushing his crew to move away from doing what he calls "gangsta shit," yet when the crew plans another crazy scheme he participates if only to protect them from themselves. For example, Fish tells Black Jesus about going over to East LA to pick up a brick for Ms. Tudi, the neighborhood drug dealer. Apparently, Ms. Tudi requested that Black Jesus drive because she trusts him. His disciples want him to come too so that he can watch over them. They hope that he will share God's good grace with them. And Fish even hints that Black Jesus might perform a miracle if they need it, but Black Jesus explains, "Man, you know I ain't in charge of the miracles, that's Pop's domain."

The show creates a parody of Jesus's struggle rebuking problematic stereotypes along the way. Satirical clashes and contradictions help the audience come to their own conclusions. In many cases, a stereotypical situation can also be empowering. For example, when the group plans a barbeque Black Jesus sends one of his disciples, Tray, to get supplies.

Tray:	"So nobody has any money for this?"
Black Jesus:	"I wanted to talk to you about that. I'm glad you brought that up. You know I love you. You know I'll never forsake you …"
Tray:	"I'm just not sure how it works without any money."
Black Jesus:	"Shhhh, all you need is the holy spirit, that's it."

Tray does return with the supplies. There is also the constant question of whether or not Black Jesus is really the Son of God. Some believe and some don't. McGruder offer clues that Jesus is real with a series of simplistic but mystical events. For example, at the barbeque Black Jesus picks up a bottle of water and miraculously it becomes a bottle of wine. This impresses his crew too much and in turn upsets Black Jesus.

> **Black Jesus:** "Is this the only way I can get ya's attention?" Come through with yak, meat and big boody women?"
> **Fish:** "It helps, nigga pour up."
> **Black Jesus:** "What happened to love and kindness? Know what I'm cool on ya. I come through spitting the gospel all the time but ya ain't trying to hear your boy. I don't even think I'm going to let you hit this fine yak cause your minds ain't ready and your hearts not open."

The storyline is designed to show how religious ideology works within this contemporary black community setting. Seeing Black Jesus use his power to help in a drug pick up or participate in growing weed at the community garden is a distorted version of religious doctrine making his involvement a complex and contradictory mode of representation. However, the participation of Black Jesus as a helpful force trying to do good offers an important discourse about how low-income black neighborhoods are too often seen as negative and worthless.

In one episode the crew drives across town to buy some weed and they are ambushed. The money is stolen and they don't get the weed. The crew chases the thieves and eventually catch them. They remove the thieves masks to discover that it is three rich white boys with fake guns. The crew takes their money back along with the weed they came to buy. They tie the boys to a fence and Black Jesus, calling each of them by name, says he wants to put his holy hands on them, but instead he is going to forgive them like his father would want.

On the way home, everyone is excited that they got to keep the money and get the weed until they are pulled over by police. When Black Jesus is yanked out of the car and slammed against the hood he yells, "I surrender, I'm not resisting." Black Jesus is the only one arrested, but he is quickly released when the police discover the package is filled with cilantro rather than weed. Soon the crew finds out that the money is gone too. Apparently, Black Jesus did not feel right stealing what he thought was real weed so he left the money with the three boys.

The rest of the first season involves Black Jesus and his disciples' efforts to start the community garden. They find a vacant lot and Ms. Tudi loans them $600 for fertilizer. However, everyone is not supportive. For example, an apartment manager, Vic, thinks Black Jesus is a con man and cult leader. On one side a Mexican gang forces the group to pay rent for the lot even though they don't own the property. On the other side Jason's girlfriend who is with the police force consistently looks for a way to arrest Black Jesus and the crew.

Throughout the adversity Black Jesus stays positive citing religious verses and singing gospel songs.

> Black Jesus: "See, open up your heart and let your boy in ... you get money f---ing with me. You ever heard of Steve Jobs, you wanna know how he made the money he gave it up to your boy. The faith of a mustard seed, of a mustard seed. That's all I ask if you gonna F--- with me you gotta believe that's all I ask." Black Jesus lifts up a huge rock and adds. "You gotta believe in somethin' why not believe in me."

Thematically, the show is designed to connect the notion of God's love for the poor with the need to believe or have faith. Black Jesus uses religious catch phrases as a defining characteristic of his powerful presence in the community. His knowledge and skills come from the Lord, so he steps over the boundaries and rationalizes his participation in the dominant street culture through God. It is an uncomfortable image for some as this kind of representation clashes between two contradictory worlds, religious and secular. However, Black Jesus is determined to make it work with his faith and miracles from "Pops."

All of the marijuana plants die in the community garden, but the green tomatoes somehow take on the same effect as weed. Black Jesus tells his crew that it is "Pops" looking out for them. Black Jesus discovers that people are getting high from God's love and grace in the tomatoes. He actually explains it more crudely. "God's love will get you f---ed up quick." The police are called to the garden and they use a dog to search for weed, but find none because all of the weed plants died. After the police leave the crew is amazed.

> Fish: "Black Jesus, I can't believe the police came to this neighborhood and actually helped us out, that's crazy."
> Black Jesus: "That's because you a disbelieving MF. You see miracles be happening in your face all the time and you don't be trying to see it."
> Maggie: "So you think God called the cops on us?'
> Black Jesus: I know he did. Dropped a dime like a straight up snitch, but you see how that shit worked out. We straight huh."
> Boonie: That MF works in mysterious ways."
> Jesus: "Yes he does."

Ms. Tudi is not simply a drug dealer, but an entrepreneur. She begins turning the tomatoes into what she sells as green ketchup and her cliental love it. Meanwhile, Vic is trying to close down the community garden to make it into a parking lot. But, Black Jesus has been so successful in getting the community to believe that they are willing to fight for the garden. Two of his crew, Fish and Maggie argue, but surprisingly Fish has also found his faith.

Fish:	"Man, Mags is trippin'. I mean what is Jesus always saying–belief, belief, belief."
Jason:	I can't believe we never got this ketchup to the market. You have no idea how good I feel right now."
Fish:	What if Martin Luther King Jr. didn't have faith? Or Nelson Mandela what if he didn't have faith?"
Boonie:	We ain't trying to be like them man. Them niggas had rough ass lives. Dogs, jail, white folks on they ass all the time. Jesus got better plans for us than that."
Fish:	Have you niggas forgot about the miracles that God has provided Already? What about them damn magic tomatoes? Or those evil-ass Mexicans that turned into nice, polite, friendly Mexicans.

During the final stand-off between the police and community members Black Jesus rides up on a horse (missing from the manure heist in an earlier episode) to turn himself in. Because the community came together in a show of collective social action to support the garden Black Jesus's faith is strengthened. When they arrest him, Jesus tells Fish, "They know not what the f- they do man. We planted the seed already, now we gotta let God do the rest. Hey, I felt that faith boy, good lookin' out." Later the community garden is destroyed and the first season ends with Black Jesus on the run. He is eventually taken to the psychiatric hospital.

In season two, Black Jesus has been caught and he is released from a psychiatric hospital. He returns to his crew who are still trying to figure out life in Compton. In the episode called "Jesus gonna get his," Black Jesus attends a nearby church with his disciples and gets very angry because the preacher is not delivering God's word correctly. Plus, he finds out that the preacher is also stealing from the tithes and offerings. Reverend Cleveland is over the top telling the congregation not to pay their bills and instead to give their money to God. He does not talk like a normal preacher and his rhetoric is extreme.

Rev. Cleveland:	"You drag your ingrate asses into this church with that 'here Jesus take this little old ten percent I got left over' and you got the nerve to wonder why your life sucks, why you ain't got shit. Keep your old funky bullshit ten percent. That's just a tip, Jesus don't want no tip. He gave you all his love, gave you all his divine grace, gave you all his salvation, and he deserves all your money."
Black Jesus:	Man that's some bullshit. He's speaking with the devil's tongue. He's trying to rip all these poor people off."

Black Jesus eventually stands up to tell the congregation that they are being ripped off which causes a change reaction as he and his crew are thrown out of the church. Later, they come up with a scheme to steal back the stolen money from the Reverend.

Every episode is sprinkled with cultural, religious and sexual contradictions. In another episode "Hands of God," God tells his son that his head has gotten too big so he wants him to wash the feet of people in the neighborhood. When Black Jesus washes Ms. Tudi's feet she gets a special feeling (it is compared to an orgasm during sex). Ms. Tudi suggests that they start a business together with Black Jesus getting paid for washing and massaging women's feet. Black Jesus is not sure this is a good idea, but Ms. Tudi asks him if God ever told him directly that he couldn't charge for his services and he replies no. The business is doing well. Women are standing in line, but Ms. Tudi gets greedy and decides to offer Fish's sexual services too. The police break up the scam before things go too far.

In the inner city there is a desperation that pushes those who want something to move across the boundaries if necessary. Black Jesus becomes the spokesperson for the poor offering a critical analysis of problems in the social system because of corrupt capitalism. We see an internal conflict as Black Jesus seeks the common good, yet he must live in a reality that is damaged. The ideological problem that is explored in the show is how this community suffers from those boundaries on both sides when it comes to religion and inner-city poverty.

Episode 11, the last episode in Season 2 is about Christmas. Black Jesus is upset because it is supposed to be a season of giving, but everybody wants something from him instead. He decides that it is his birthday and to celebrate it he is going to resist the oppressive social holiday that Christmas has become. First, he has a run in with a nonbeliever, Vic, that sets him off.

Vic:	I've got some good news for you man. A gift straight from God."
Black Jesus:	What? Hey Pops blessed you with a gift? The word? Aww man, that's the gift that keeps on giving. Come on lay it on me. What did He say?"
Vic:	"He said, 'Beware of false prophets, those that would disguise themselves to be servants of righteousness. The end will correspond with their deeds, as they will be hurled into a lake of burning sulfur to be tormented day in and day out forever"

(Matthew 7: 15 and Revelation 20:10).

Black Jesus is more depressed after his meeting with Vic. He goes to the apartment of his disciple Fish.

Black Jesus:	"Man seriously though, whatever that is out there everybody celebrating ain't got shit to do with me."
Jason:	"Yeah, yeah yeah, we know Jesus you hate Christmas."
Fish:	"Everybody knows that you hate Christmas."
Boonie:	"Man why you got to f- it up for the rest of us. You want to be known as the Jesus that ruined Christmas?"
Fish:	Don't be ruining our Christmas just because you in a bad mood. We gonna celebrate your birthday a little early this year."

Jason hands Black Jesus a large blunt and Boonie opens up his jacket to show Jesus what he has written on his tee-shirt "Happy Birthday Jesus."

Black Jesus smiles but continues to protest an indifferent world that has moved away from celebrating his birth the way they are supposed to. Later at the mall, a little kid is excited to see Black Jesus, but Black Jesus is still despondent.

Kid:	Hey Jesus what am I getting this year?
Black Jesus:	Nothing man, your daddy is an alcoholic and lost his job. Stop being so self-centered. The kid cries.
Maggie:	Jesus you shouldn't do stuff like that.
Black Jesus:	No, they don't care about nothing but themselves.
Maggie:	People are over Christmas now. You're not the only one who hates your birthday. If you don't have a job, you don't have no money, you can't go shopping. To be honest we all wish we could skip it.
Black Jesus:	And I wish I could just skip being the holy redeemer and the heavenly savior.
Maggie:	Alright, now you talking crazy.
Black Jesus:	No, I'm telling the truth, man. Sometimes I don't even want to be Jesus no more. Here I am spreading the goodness and the M'F' light, you feel me? That's all I got, but all they know is this Santa Clause bullshit."

Black Jesus destroys the Santa Clause display in the department store and the security guard knocks him unconscious. While he is out he experiences the *Christmas Carol* story seeing how everyone in Compton is impacted differently without him around. When he wakes up he is happy to be Black Jesus again.

Black Jesus:	"At the end of it all what matters most is me, Jesus Christ. As much as I loved me before I love me even more now. And that's what Christmas is all about. F--- Santa Clause!"

Throughout the series Black Jesus expresses anger about society's transgressions, while accepting everyone as the imperfect people they are. He also articulates the word within specific boundaries highlighting individual ideas of morality and difference. In *Black Jesus* the connection between race, class, and religion is used to question humanity as it exists today. The hypocrisy of today's society is an important dialogue that McGruder wanted his work to inspire.

References

Adams, D. T. (2018, January 31). The portrayal of Africa and Africans in the book of Jeremiah. *AOSIS*. Retrieved from: https://indieskriflig.org.za/index.php/skriflig/ article/view/2259/4920

Adams-Bass, V., Stevensen, H., & Korzin D. (2014). Measuring the meaning of black media stereotypes and their relationship to the racial identity, black history knowledge and racial socialization of African American youth. *Journal of Black Studies, 45*(5), 367–395.

Beckson, K., & Ganz, A. (1989). *Literary terms: A dictionary*. New York, NY: Noonday.

Braxton, G. (2014, August 7). 'Black Jesus' comes in peace, according to his formerly angry creator. *Los Angeles Times*. Retrieved from http://www.latimes.com/ entertainment/tv/la-et-st-black-jesus-aaron-mcgruder-20140807-story.html

Bryson, B., & Davis, A. (2010). Conquering stereotypes in research on race and gender. *Sociological Forum, 25*(1), 161–166.

Callahan, L. (2014, August 8). *Black Jesus*: We have other things to boycott. *Time.com*. Retrieved from http://time.com/3092051/black-jesus-boycott/

Cone, J. (2010). *A black theology of liberation*. Maryknoll, NY: Orbis Books.

De Moraes, L. (2014, July 24). Christian group blasts Adult Swim's '*Black Jesus*' to surprise of no one. *Deadline Hollywood*. Retrieved from https://deadline.com/ 2014/07/christian-group-blasts-adult-swims-black-jesus-to-surprise-of-no-one-video-809032/

Diamant, J. (2018, May 7). Blacks more likely than others to read God's word, see it as God's word. *Pew Research Center, Fact Think Tank*. Retrieved from http://www.pewresearch.org/fact-tank/2018/05/07/blacks-more-likely-than-others-in-u-s-to-read-the-bible-regularly-see-it-as-gods-word/

Dickson-Carr, D. (2001). *African American satire: The sacredly profane novel*. Columbia, MO: University of Missouri Press.

Douglas, M. (2002). *Purity and danger: An analysis of concepts of pollution and taboo*. New York, NY: Praeger. (Originally published 1966)

Epstein, C. (1992). Tinkerbells and pinups: The construction and reconstruction of gender boundaries at work. In M. Lamont & M. Fournier (Eds.), *Cultivating differences: Symbolic boundaries and the making of inequality* (pp. 232–256). Chicago, IL: University of Chicago Press.

Epstein, C. (2010). On boundaries. *Sociological Forum, 25*(1), 148–160.

Feldman, J. (2014, July 29). *CNN's* Lemon on Black Jesus uproar: Don't be so sensitive, have a sense of humor. *Mediaite*. Retrieved from https://www.mediaite.com/ online/cnns-lemon-on-black-jesus-uproar-dont-be-so-sensitive-have-a-sense-of-humor/

Gallop, J. D. (2014), Aug 6. '*Black Jesus*' raises ire of pastors, faith groups. *USA Today*. Retrieved from https://www.usatoday.com/story/news/nation/2014/08/06/black-jesus-raises-ire-pastors-faith-groups/13655537/

Gilmore, J., & Jordan, A. (2012, April). Burgers and basketball: Race and stereotypes in food and beverage advertising aimed at children in the US. *Journal of Children and Media*, 6(3), 317–332.

Gray, H. (2005). *Cultural Moves: African Americans and the politics of representation*. Berkley: University of California Press.

Hays, J. D. (2003). *From every people and nation: A biblical theology of race*. Downers Grove, IL: Inter Varsity Press Academic.

Hodge, S., Burden, J., Robinson, L., & Bennett, R. (2008). Theorizing on the stereotyping of black male athletes. *Journal for the Study of Sports and Athletes in Education*, 2(2), 203–226.

Holman, C., & Harmon, W. (1992). *A handbook to literature*. New York, NY: Macmillan.

Kreuz, R., & Roberts, R. (1993). On satire and parody: The importance of being ironic. *Metaphor and Symbol*, 8(2), 97–109.

Loury, B. (2014, August 6). TV review: Black Jesus. *Variety*. Retrieved from https://variety.com/2014/tv/reviews/tv-review-black-jesus-1201276024/

Masci, D. (2018, February 7). 5 Facts about the religious lives of African Americans. *Pew Research Center, Fact think Tank*. Retrieved from http://www.pewresearch.org/fact-tank/2018/02/07/5-facts-about-the-religious-lives-of-african-americans/

McClennen, S. (2019, February 23). 5 ways the 2020 election will be shaped by late night comedy. *Salon*. Retrieved from https://www.salon.com/2019/02/23/5-ways-the-2020-election-will-be-shaped-by-late-night-comedy/

McClennen, S., & Maisel, R. (2014). *Is satire saving our nation: Mockery and politics*. New York, NY: Palgrave Macmillan.

One Million Moms. (2018, April 9). After a skipped season *"Black Jesus"* is back. Retrieved from https://onemillionmoms.com/current-campaigns/after-a-skipped-season-black-jesus-is-back/

Sanders, M., & Ramasubramanian, S. (2012, January). An examination of African American's stereotyped perceptions of fictional media characters. *Howard Journal of Communication*, 23(1), 17–39.

Schaffner, B., & Gadson, M. (2004). Reinforcing stereotypes? Race and local television news coverage of Congress. *Social Science Quarterly*, 85(3), 604–623.

Sewell, C. (2013). Mammies and matriarchs: Tracing images of the black female in popular culture 1950's to present. *Journal of African American Studies*, 17, 308–326.

Tyree, T. (2011). African American Stereotypes in Reality Television, *Howard Journal of Communications*, 22(4), 394–413.

Wayne, M. (2017, January 30). Jesus is black, get over it. *Premier Christianity*. Retrieved from https://www.premierchristianity.com/Blog/Jesus-is-black.-Get-over-it

Welch, K. (2007). Black criminal stereotypes and racial profiling. *Journal of Contemporary Criminal Justice*, 23(3), 276–288.

CHAPTER SEVEN

Deconstructing Intersectionality in *Crash*

With a 6.5 million dollar budget, *Crash* (2004) grossed almost 100 million dollars worldwide after its release in May of 2005 (Jacobs, 2017). It garnered six Oscar nominations, and eventually won three for Best Picture, Best Editing, and Best Original Screenplay (Caro, 2006). In an interview with director Matthew Jacobs the co-writer Paul Haggis discussed how being from Canada allowed him to see small contrasts and comparisons concerning attitudes and behaviors among different races and classes in Los Angeles that many others often missed. Haggis said he purposefully pushed stereotypical roles for the first twenty minutes of the movie and then turned them around (Jacobs, 2017).

> I wanted people to relax and say, I'm not going to challenge you. I'm only going to reinforce every stereotype you ever thought and let you laugh at it. And then as soon as I've got you relaxed, I can start twisting you around in your seat until you're left spinning.

The movie begins and ends with a car crash. In the beginning, a voiceover by police detective Graham says, "It's the sense of touch. In a real city you walk. You brush past people. People bump into you. In LA nobody touches you. We're always behind metal and glass. I think we miss that touch so much that we crash into something just so we can feel something."

Crash shows how people from different cultures and ideologies are colliding with each other every day in the city of Los Angeles. There is a large ensemble cast including many well-known celebrities such as Sandra Bullock, Terrence Howard, Don Cheadle, Ludacris, Lorenz Tate, Matt Dillon, Thandie Newton, Loretta Devine and others. Anthony and Peter are black male carjackers. Graham, black, and Ria, Puerto Rican, are partners and lovers in the LA police department, plus Graham is Peter's older brother. Jean and Rick are an upper class, white married couple. Rick is the city's district attorney and Jean doesn't work. Dorri works at a hospital and her father, Farhad owns his own store. Their family is from Persia, but people think they are Arab and constantly harass them because of 9/11. Daniel is a LatinX locksmith who moved his family into a better neighborhood after a stray bullet flew through the daughter's window. Ryan and Tommy are white police officers. Ryan is a veteran officer who is racist and sexist while Tommy is a new officer who is idealistic about the role of police in Los Angeles. Cameron and his wife Christine are both black. Cameron is a Hollywood director and his wife Christine doesn't work. Finally, Totinko is literally run over by the carjackers, Anthony and Peter, and he ends up in the hospital before he can deliver the group of illegal immigrants that he was paid to pick up.

This twisted storyline in *Crash* connects through various real, symbolic and ideological intersections in an effort to disturb and challenge our perceptions of societal institutions, as well as individual, and collective behaviors (Goodall, Good and Godfrey, 2007).

> Haggis constructs representations of intolerance amongst and reconciliation between, the various ethnicities in order to illuminate issues of authority between the inter-race and inter-class relationships among the professionals of the political, law enforcement, health and media worlds, among the out of town, would be gangsters displaced within white terrain, among recent and longstanding immigrants, and among other groups whose illegal immigration is either willing or enforced. (p. X)

Intersectionality

Established by Crenshaw (1989), Intersectionality was designed to assess multiple constructions of identity in the social world. Specifically, she wanted to help researchers understand that a single axis framework when it comes to black women was inadequate. For example, feminism's focus on white women and anti-racism's focus on black men tends to erase the importance of black women. Her work also explored the position of class in analytical constructions, particularly the privileged versus poor classes.

In an article on the rape and the battering of women of color, Crenshaw (1991) expands her notion of intersectionality further to include structural intersectionality (location), political intersectionality (marginalization) and representational (cultural) intersectionality. She believes if intersectionality is not taken into consideration during any analysis of people of color it can lead to deletion and/or disempowerment.

According to Delgado and Stefancic (2001) intersectionality involves a number of categories.

> the examination of race, sex, class, national origin and sexual orientation and how their combination plays out in various settings. These categories and still others can be separate disadvantaging factors. (p. 51)

Both argue that these categories as subgroups can determine who has power and voice and who does not. Rigoni (2012) focuses on how intersectionality can recognize multidimensional identities as well, she believes they are constructed in flux through the process of hybridity and within spaces of belonging. In her research, Rigoni explores how the participation of ethnic minorities in media products often challenges complex power relations associated with race, class, and gender.

This complexity involves for McCall (2005) the inclusion of multiple intersections and social relations. She argues that deconstructing normative categorical assumptions can ultimately contribute to the possibility of positive social change. "The categorical approach focuses on the complexity of relationships among multiple social groups within and across analytical categories and not on complexities within single social groups, single categories or both" (p. 1786).

In order to account for the diversity of experience, McCall offers three additional concepts to consider anticategorical, intracategorical, and intercategorical complexity. Anticategorical complexity suggests that social life is too fluid and intricate to have fixed categories. Intracategorical complexity examines multiple and conflicting categories across various groups. Intercategorical complexity involves the various categories found within various groups. *Crash* acknowledges the intersectionality and d complexity of every day existence.

Deconstruction

As Norris (2004) suggests the perplexities of meaning, intent and voice are important as a metaphor of truth and authenticity in deconstruction.

> ...deconstruction is not simply a strategic reversal of categories which otherwise remain distinct and unaffected. It seeks to undo both a given order of priorities and the very system of conceptual opposition that make that order possible. (p. 31)

Taguchi (2010) explains Derrida's deconstructive theory (1976, 1981) as rethinking a concept so that it is no longer a representation of the real and it does not necessarily carry its own meaning. It is seen instead in relation to other concepts around it. For instance, binaries like man/woman, upper class/lower class, or black/white serve as important oppositional meanings and distinguishing truths.

> It is a strategy that can only be done with and from within the set of meanings present in the text and the absences they rely on. This strategy of disruption and interference, with settled oppositions and dominant meanings also aims to trace the limits and power producing effects of these meanings and binaries? (p. 44)

Hill-Collins and Bilge (2016) argue that intersectionality can be used effectively as an analytic tool to explore complex differences including such binaries.

> Intersectionality is a way of understanding and analyzing the complexity in the world, in people and in human experiences. The events and conditions of social and political life and the self can seldom be understood as shaped by one factor. They are generally shaped by many factors in diverse and mutually influencing ways. When it comes to social inequality, people's lives and the organization of power in a given society are better understood as being shaped not by single axis of social division, be it race or gender or class, but by many axes that work together and influence each other. (p. 2)

In other words, all meaning involves negotiated discourses around embedded multiplicities and the deconstruction of a text can help to better understand how these related discourses operate. This means that social, historical, linguistic, political, gendered, racial, and other identities must be connected and cannot be ignored.

Deconstruction, Intersectionality, and *Crash*

Crash offers a broad range of intersectional frameworks. Hill-Collins and Bilge describe four domains of intersectional power, interpersonal, disciplinary, cultural and structural. The goal of this chapter is to deconstruct exemplars in *Crash* in relation to these four intersectional domains of power, specifically using elements surrounding race.

Interpersonal power is perpetuated by most of the characters in the movie. One of the primary police officers, Ryan is depicted as a racist and sexist cop.

When he pulls over Cameron and Christine he knows that they are not the suspects described in a call from dispatch, but he is looking for a racial target. Christine does not listen to Ryan when he tells her to be quiet and stay in the car. Instead, she gets out and harasses Ryan. Ryan pushes her up against the car and under the guise of checking for weapons feels all over her body. Ryan's actions are aggressive in relation to interpersonal power because as a police officer he feels that he is above the law. At the same time, Ryan's actions can also be seen as part of a structural domain of power over black people which is one reason why many police departments have a tense and troubling relationship with the black community.

Prejudice is a pattern found throughout the storyline of *Crash* and an integral part of the interpersonal domain of power. The character of Jean is married to the Los Angeles district attorney. Even though as a white woman she should understand the insult of being judged at least by gender, she does not take that into account when she makes negative statements about the two black carjackers, her immigrant maid or the LatinX locksmith. As a wealthy white woman, she has the luxury of remaining separated from inequality by her white privilege.

Name calling and broad societal assumptions also display various interpersonal domains of power. The Asian lady who gets into a car accident is accused of not being able to drive, the assumption that the name Shaniqua means the black woman is ignorant, confusing LatinX ethnicities such as Puerto Ricans, Mexicans, and Cubans, plus the black lieutenant in the police force telling Tommy that he had to work hard as a black man to get to where he is in a racist organization like the LAPD and it can easily be taken away.

Interpersonal redemption is also used as a layer of intersectional complexity in *Crash*. The most prominent example occurs when the racist, sexist police officer later saves the life of the same woman that he felt up in the traffic stop. There is an accident and Christine's car has flipped over. She is trapped inside with gas leaking and fire inching closer. At first, when she sees that her rescuer is Ryan she fights him, but soon Christine realizes that she is in real trouble and allows him help. Ultimately, they must cling to each other in order to escape.

In another example, the upper-class white female, Jean admits on the phone to a friend that she is angry all the time and she doesn't know why. Then when she falls down her steps and twists her ankle she can't get help from any of her friends. It is her maid who takes her to the hospital. Jean hugs the woman tightly and tells her, "You're the best friend I've got."

A traffic accident involving an Asian man who is getting out of his van offers a third example. Peter argues with Anthony who insists that they can't leave the man on the street and let him die. So, they load him into the car and literally dump his body in front of a hospital. Later Anthony is walking past the same van and sees that the keys are still in the outside lock. He drives the van to the chop shop and discovers scared illegal Cambodian immigrants in the back. The owner of the chop shop offers to buy the people, but Anthony refuses. Instead he drops them off in China Town and gives them forty dollars for food, all of the money he has in his pocket.

An interesting look at the disciplinary domain of power involves the idea that whiteness is equal to success and people of color are often treated differently as a result. When Cameron, a black male director is told by his white producer that the black character in their television show is not talking black enough, Cameron is unable to object. He must stand by and be humiliated because blacks are expected to speak, dress and act in a stereotypical way in order to be considered truly black. Cameron struggles with the fact that he does not have the power to change things. In his analysis of *Crash*, Holmes (2007) suggests that the black characters have agency over their own voices, until the whites in charge decide otherwise. This infers the presence of a white structural domain of power at work.

Disciplinary intersectionality can trigger discrimination that influences the treatment of different people. For instance, while Daniel is changing the locks, Jean tells her husband that Daniel is going to sell their key to his gangbanger friends so she wants the locks changed again in the morning. As a LatinX locksmith, Daniel may look like a typical gangbanger (tattoos and shaved head), but he is in fact a loving husband and father. This movie challenges the normalized stereotypes by placing Daniel, who may look like a thug, in a job as a locksmith where he is responsible for securing safety. It is an interesting twist that shows us how structural domains of power can be tenuous.

Another interesting disciplinary twist involves the good police officer Tommy. He is a young, naïve officer offended by Ryan's racist and sexist actions, so he requests to ride by himself. On his way home that night after work he picks up Peter who is hitchhiking. In their conversation, Tommy doesn't believe that Peter as a young black man enjoys country music and ice skates. When Peter notices a St. Christopher statue on Tommy's dash he begins to laugh, Tommy thinks Peter is laughing at him. He stops the car to put Peter out, and when Peter attempts to pull out the St. Christopher statue that he carries in his pocket to show Tommy what he is actually laughing about Tommy thinks Peter is reaching for a gun and shoots. Rather than report the murder, Tommy drags Peter's body out of the car and into a tall grassy area on the side of the road, then drives his car to a vacant lot and sets it on fire.

The Persian family that owns a neighborhood store in the film are treated as potential terrorists. When the shop is broken into the father, Farhad, buys a gun for protection. The locksmith Daniel had tried to fix the lock earlier and warned the father that the back door needed to be replaced because the lock wouldn't hold, but Farhad did not listen. When his daughter Dorri goes with Farhad to buy the gun she tries to talk him out of it. The father is offended by the gun store owner and they start to argue, so the daughter sends her father outside to finalize the transaction. The daughter selects a box of blanks for the gun rather than actual bullets because she doesn't know the difference. When the father in his anger later tries to shoot Daniel blaming him for the insurance company's decision not to pay for the break in at the store no one is hurt because he shoots a blank. The scene is made even more intense when Daniel's daughter runs out of the house and jumps into his arms just as the gun goes off. Farhad calls her his angel.

An exploration of cultural power through intersectionality in *Crash* explains how the story is able to create complex and interesting characters beyond stereotypes. The movie effectively uses the metaphor of 'crash' to critique certain racial, social, and political ideologies. For example, the car jackers Anthony and Peter are introduced after eating dinner at a restaurant in an upper-class white neighborhood. Anthony is a criminal, but he is also an urban philosopher constantly spouting street wisdom. For example, he explains numerous cultural positions such as black people steal from each other because they are scared of white people, the big windows on a bus are designed to humiliate the people of color who must ride busses, Hip Hop is the music of the oppressor pushing nigga this and nigga that, and most black men look like gangbangers to most white people simply because of the color of their skin.

The *Crash* storyline provides other examples of race and its relationship to the cultural domain of power by contrasting good against bad. First, Peter and Graham were raised in the same household in Compton. Yet, Peter is one of the carjackers and Graham is a police detective. Their mother is a drug addict who worries about Peter and blames Graham when his brother is killed. Second, the black television director is carjacked by Anthony and in the struggle Cameron takes away Anthony's gun. As a police car approaches, Anthony jumps into the passenger seat and slides down, while Cameron drives away. At the end of a chase they are surrounded by police officers with guns pulled. Cameron is obviously on edge. He has had an argument with his wife Christine who accused him of not protecting her from the cop who felt her up, his producer challenged his understanding of blackness, and there is also the obvious tension between police and black men in general. The compassionate white officer, Tommy calms things down and once the stand-off with police is over Cameron is allowed to drive away. He stops several blocks away, gives Anthony his gun back and tells him to get out of his car. Then before Anthony walks away Cameron tells him, "You embarrass me, you embarrass yourself."

The structural domain of power is also evident after Anthony and Peter carjack Jean and her husband Rick at gun point. Rick is the city's district attorney so this action kicks off a series of events that leaves the DA's office focusing on damage control. Rick's office is in turmoil because it is an election year and he needs the black vote to win. There is a second controversial racial incident that adds to the structural chaos and Rick's team must try to spin this situation as well. A black police officer is shot by a white police officer and both were undercover and off duty. This is the third black person the white officer has shot in several months. Ultimately, despite the fact that the black officer had $300,000 hidden in the truck of his car and was possibly high on drugs, Rick's team coerces Graham, the black detective on the case, with a deal. They will erase his brother's record if he pushes the DA's story that a racist white cop shot a black, off-duty officer. The DA's campaign can use that story to garner black votes.

According to Holmes (2007), *Crash* blurs the distinction between individual moral choices and larger institutional practices. Holmes adds that even without intending to, the writers of *Crash* indirectly conflate race with racism. That is where racialism comes in. Of course, a portion of this film is about racism, but it also includes many viable examples of racialism. Because of institutional white privilege and progressive white identity, people of color exist on the margins of the mainstream. Society constantly experiences crashes between cultures when it comes to what is believed and valued.

Carbado, Crenshaw, Mays, and Tomlinson (2013), have found that intersectionality consists of a range of cultural issues, social identities, power dynamics, societal systems, and institutional structures. They describe the process of intersectionality as an analysis in progress. It crosses multiple disciplines, encompasses national and international discourses, engages a wide range of experiences, identifies relevant structures of power, and ultimately creates a movement toward social change.

Crash demonstrates various ways that racialism is integrated into the fabric of society based on interpersonal, disciplinary, cultural, and structural domains of power. Intersectionality serves as a powerful element of discourse in this film confronting the stereotypical ideology as it ruptures fixed categories related to the complexity of life.

References

Carbado, D., Crenshaw, K., Mays, V., & Tomlinson, B. (2013). Intersectionality: Mapping the movements of a theory. *DuBois Review, 10*(2), 303–312.

Caro, M. (2006, February 12). From crazy idea to the Oscars: The journey of *Crash*. *Chicago Tribune*. Retrieved from https://www.chicagotribune.com/news/ct-xpm-2006-02-12-0602120059-story.html

Crash. IMDb. Retrieved from https://www.imdb.com/title/tt0375679/

Crenshaw, K. (1989). Demarginalizing the intersection of race and sex: A black feminist critique of anti-discrimination doctrine, Feminist Theory and anti-racist politics. *University of Chicago Legal Forum, 1*(8), 139–167.

Crenshaw, K. (1991, July). Mapping the margins: Intersectionality, identity politics, and violence against women of color. *Stanford Law Review, 43*(6), 1241–1299.

Delgado, R., & Stefancic, J. (2001). *Critical Race Theory: An introduction*. New York: New York University Press.

Derrida, J. (1976). *Of grammatology*. Baltimore, MA: The John Hopkins University Press.

Derrida, J. (1981). *Positions*. London, England: The Athlone Press.

Goodall, M., Good, J., & Godfrey, W. (2007). *Crash cinema: Representation in film*. Newcastle, England: Cambridge Scholars Publishing.

Hill-Collins, P., & Bilge, S. (2016). *Intersectionality: Key Concepts*. Cambridge, MA: Polity Press.

Holmes, D. (2007, March). The Civil Rights Movement according to *Crash*: Complicating the pedagogy of integration. *College English, 69*(4), 314–320.

Jacobs, M. (2017, December 6). A decade after *Crash*, Paul Haggis reflects on the polarizing racial fable that stormed the Oscars. *Huffpost*. Retrieved from https://www.huffingtonpost.com/2015/05/06/paul-haggis-crash_n_7216026.html

McCall, L. (2005, Spring). The complexity of intersectionality. *Signs, Journal of Women in Culture and Society, 30*(3), 1771–1800.

Norris, C. (2004). *Deconstruction: Theory and Practice*. New York, NY: Routledge.

Rigoni, I. (2012). Intersectionality and mediated cultural production in a globalized post-colonial world. *Ethnic and Racial Studies, 35*(5), 834–849.

Taguchi, H. (2010). Doing collaborative deconstruction as an exorbitant strategy in qualitative research. *Reconceptualizing Educational Research Methodology, 1*(1), 41–53.

CHAPTER EIGHT

Black Twitter, Interpretive Communities, and Cultural Capital

In her paper, "Whose Culture has Capital?" Yosso (2005) challenges the traditional top down interpretation of cultural capital to argue instead for a bottom up notion of community cultural wealth. Based on Critical Race Theory, her goal is to draw on the knowledge and strength that people of color encompass in the fight for social and racial justice. This chapter explores Yosso's idea as an essential part of Black Twitter which has quickly become an inspiration for community cultural capital across the United States and around the world.

For many years black people were considered lacking in social and cultural capital. The cultural capital theory proposed by Pierre Bourdieu (Bourdieu & Passeron, 1979) suggested that as a hierarchical society the upper and middle classes were more valuable than the lower class. Social media has turned that idea upside down with Black Twitter emerging as a powerful and effective tool for communication and resistance. In 2002, Franklin defined cultural capital as, "a sense of group consciousness and collective identity that serves as a resource aimed at the advancement of the entire group" (p. 177).

Interpretive Communities

Black Twitter challenges normal communication pathways shaping an empowered interpretive community. The idea of "interpretive community" as a place for shared meaning and social interaction has been presented by scholars like Fish (1980), Radway (1984), Jensen (1991), Zelizer (1993), Berkowitz and TerKeurst (1999). Schroder (1994) added depth to the notion when he layered interpretive communities with the concept of situationism. He noted that situationism is important when examining interpretive communities since most people use social media in specific situations.

As early as 1980, Hymes defined interpretive community as a group united by a shared notion of reality. Community members create, interpret, and respond to texts based on certain common conventions according to Coyle and Lindlof (1988). Zelizer (1993) suggested that journalistic interpretive communities share discourse and collective interpretations about public events. Finally, Jensen (1990) discusses the interpretive ability of an audience to critique television.

> First, the word interpretive implies that audiences, while being demographic entities also make up cultural formations, whose interpretive strategies in relation to mass media give rise to different constructions of social reality ... Second, the word communities indicates that audiences may also constitute social agents with shared interests, or publics. (p. 130)

Beck (1995) and Liebes and Katz (1990) examine how shared interpretations emerge from a text through member interaction. Aden, Rahoi, and Beck (1995) explain the process of interpretation as empowering because it enables interpretive communities through popular texts to better engage in the culture in which they live. And in his dissertation on black interpretive communities and the electronic church, Mitchell (2005) found that para-social interactions with televangelists can create interpretive communities where the individual's social and cultural context is extended beyond viewing to include other outside encounters and contacts.

Black Twitter

A significant amount of research has been conducted on Black Twitter. The findings by Fox, Zickuhr, and Smith (2009) showed that Twitter is used by African Americans more than any other group. Dixon (2011) argued that social media plays a prominent role in promoting relevant causes for blacks and Hispanics. Hill's research (1995) demonstrated that most social media contexts use whites as the invisibly normal while racialized populations become visibly marginal. And, according to Brock (2012) Black Twitter actually encourages increased participation when it comes to cultural communication.

> Black hashtag signifying revealed alternate Twitter discourses to the mainstream and encouraged formulations of Black Twitter as a social public; a community constructed through their use of social media by out-siders and insiders alike. (p. 530)

From the same article, Brock defined Black Twitter as, "a user generated source of culturally relevant online content, combining social network elements and broadcast principles to share information" (p. 530). He believes that today hashtag Black Twitter offers an alternative to mainstream ideas and trends because culture shapes online conversations and the designated hashtag encourages participants to respond.

> I found that a tweet's content coupled with a topical hashtag, when leavened with cultural commonplaces, could enrich communal bonds between networked Twitter users; this happens regardless of cultural affiliation. (p. 644)

Clark (2014) in her dissertation explored the multi-level community network encompassed by Black Twitter. She ultimately documented that among Black Twitter users there are several things going on at the same time including: engagement and community building, challenging normalized social identity, and socially constructing an identifiable, influential meta-network of cultural communicators.

Social and political causes are some of the most popular Black Twitter pursuits. The hashtag for #BlackLivesMatter in 2015 remains one of the top ten trending topics in the case study by McDaniels (2017). Her dissertation examined the nature of social sharing, emotion and self-expression to find that 65% of #BlackLivesMatter tweets were supportive. Focusing on the death of Michael Brown, a study by Ray, Brown, Fraistat, and Summers (2017) identified the evolution of collective identities through Black Twitter. They cited the two most prominent hashtags as one that was supportive from #Blacklivesmatter and the other oppositional from #TCOT (Top Conservatives on Twitter).

The construction of racial identity using Black Twitter was studied by Harlow and Benbrook (2017). Their findings demonstrated how Hip Hop celebrities helped to enhance black identity and also helped build the #BlackLivesMatter movement. The study cited four identity themes: (1) speaking to whites, (2) solidarity among participants, (3) Black is beautiful, and (4) the importance of equality. When Baldridge (2014) explored how black youth are using Black Twitter and other social media, he found that they are challenging and transgressing those narratives that suggest they are inherently violent, criminal, and disposable. And finally, Black Twitter's role in creating a digital counter-public was examined by Hill (2018). Hill explained that as a counter-public Black Twitter enables, "critical pedagogy, political organizing, and both symbolic and material forms of resistance to address anti-black state violence within the United States."

Ince, Rojas, and Davis (2017) asked an important question in their research on the response to the Black Lives Matter movement - how do online communities like Black Twitter influence the framing of such a movement? Their study reported that several prominent themes were connected to Black Twitter. Those themes included, solidarity or the approval of the movement, an end to police violence, understanding movement tactics, details about Ferguson, and a look at counter movement opportunities. #BlackLivesMatter has also used social media to organize, protest and create awareness according to Byrd, Gilbert, and Richardson (2017). They suggest that more researchers must study the implications of activism through social media to learn how it plays a role in social change.

Black Twitter offers a significant cultural text that enables socially constructed and shared meanings. It is obvious that participants through consumption engage in both critique and comradery. Participants take the opportunity to use this resource for conversation and debate about black issues. Gray (1989) believes that the struggle for relevant communication in black communities is essential. Black Twitter is an answer that struggle. Cultural hashtags on the social media site allow for relevant issues to become significant trending topics to an eager public.

Trending Topics

Situations are shaped and processed through Black Twitter as meaningful cultural texts. The use of popular hashtags like #BlackLivesMatter, #BlackGirlMagic, #TweetLikethe1600s, #StayMadAbby, #LemonadeSyllabus, #DonLemonLogic, #BlackPanther, #WakandaForever, #OscarsSoWhite, and many others quickly become part of public cultural discourse. Participants on Black Twitter are able to build enhanced communication sites that enable them to challenge issues, offer knowledge and support each other. In the more than ten years that Black Twitter has been in existence below are exemplars of a few topics that have gone viral.

BLACK TWITTER, INTERPRETIVE COMMUNITIES, AND CULTURAL CAPITAL | 113

#BlackLivesMatter

By all accounts the top hashtag has been #BlackLivesMatter. It was a response to the death of Trayvon Martin, an unarmed 17-year-old who was murdered by George Zimmerman in 2012 (Mone, 2017). According to Mone, it was created by Alicia Garza, Patrisse Cullors, and Opal Tometi in 2013, and by July of that same year the hashtag was appearing on Twitter about 30 times a day. This hashtag has since connected to a series of murders where black men and women were killed by police and others without consequence including: Michael Brown, Sandra Bland, Freddy Gray, Eric Garner, Tamir Rice, and Stephon Clark (Taylor, 2016). Selected examples of #BlackLivesMatter tweets include:

@Blklivesmatter

BLM is an affirmation & embrace of the resistance & resilience of black people. Founded by @osopepatrisse @opalayo@aliciagarza …

Nathan H. Rubin @NathanHRubin Apr 24

Tamir Rice—playing on a playground; shot twice. Dylan Roof—known mass murderer; arrested peacefully. Stephon Clark—in a backyard holding a cell phone; shot 20 times. Waffle House Shooter—known mass murderer; arrested peacefully. Get it yet? **#BlackLivesMatter**

JERSEYCRAIG @CJPatruno Apr 22

When you speak to someone who gets mad about the name of the **#BlackLivesMatter** movement, just show them this. More than likely they still won't understand but maybe they will think for a moment.

Shaun King Verified account @ShaunKing Apr 23

Dear America, what we are basically asking is for African Americans to be treated by police with the respect, dignity, and safety that is so often afforded to heavily armed white mass murderers. **#BlackLivesMatter**

DanielleMoodie-Mills Verified account @DeeTwoCents May 20

DanielleMoodie-Mills Retweeted Shomari Stone

Another white guy with a gun murders police officer but TAKEN ALIVE INTO CUSTODY. Let that sink in when you want to debate me on **#BlackLivesMatter** How do white police officers not "fear for their lives" when white CRIMINALS have guns?! But black kid on a playground is fair game?

CRMC @CivilRightsCntr May 20

Happy Birthday, Michael Brown. In 2014, Brown, an unarmed black teenager, was fatally shot twelve times in Ferguson, MO. The incident ignited protests around the country, but the officer who killed Brown was never prosecuted. **#RestInPower#TheMarchContinues #BlackLivesMatter**

G @burnerama3 Apr 23

Kanye West just did more for the black community than all of Black Lives Matter Marches combined with a radio interview and a few tweets. Progressive thinker. #KanyeWest **#BlackLivesMatter** #maga #potus #hot97 #usa #Kanye2024 3 replies 51 retweets 141 likes

te @CateCosburn 54m54 minutes ago
Stare at me while I shop for no reason. Call the police for no reason. Hurt/Kill me for no reason. Hate me for no reason. Expecting me to let this continue? UNREASONABLE.

patrisse cullors Verified account @OsopePatrisse May 22
https://deadline.com/2019/05/good-trouble-patrisse-cullors-writers-room-season-2-1202620887/ ... they said @Blklivesmatter would only be a fad. Well we in the writers room baby! Thank you @GoodTrouble @FreeformTV and @JoannaJohnson31 for seeing the value in black activist storylines! **#BlackLivesMatter**

#BlackPanther, #WakandaForever

Black Panther quickly became one of the highest grossing films ever passing the billion-dollar mark in just one month. *Entertainment Weekly* reported that with 35 million tweets *Black Panther* climbed to the top film platform on Twitter (Holub, 2018). It is the fantasy of how an African society from the land of Wakanda is enriched by a vein of vibranium which enables them to develop high-tech healthcare, transportation, and weapondry. In *Time Magazine*, Smith (2018) argues that making movies about black lives is key to showing that they matter. He notes in this post-Obama era *Black Panther* was truly groundbreaking.

> In the midst of a regressive culture and political movement fueled in part by the white-nativist movement, the very existence of *Black Panther* feels like resistance. Its themes challenge institutional bias, its characters take unsubtle digs at oppressors, and its narrative includes prismatic perspectives on black life and tradition. (Smith, 2018)

Selected examples of #BlackPanther and #WakandaForever tweets include:
FohloZa @FareedahMoosa Apr 23
I still want to know why none of the fast food chains had any **#BlackPanther** toys given with the kiddies meals 😒 😒
Alpha Wolf @King__Jaydn
The only time Black Americans remember to support the motherland is #BlackHistoryMonth 👣 and when #BlackPanther 🐱 is on TV. A lot of you don't even know Africa is a whole ass Continent not a country 🤦 4:45 AM—28 Apr 2018

THE GLAMAHOLIC @JaylaKoriyan 2h2 hours ago

Seeing the strength and power of the #WomenOfWakanda in the film @BlackPanther showed so much empowerment for women. Bring home **#BlackPanther** on Digital May 8 and Blu-ray May 15! #ad

Cuiet(4.26) @Cuiet426 21h21 hours ago

Long Live the king ... **#BlackPanther** 🐱 #streetart #graffiti

W @tweetticator 24h24 hours ago

"We all know the truth: more connects us than separates us. But in times of crisis, the wise build bridges while the foolish build barriers. We must find a way to look after one another as if we were one single tribe."—Ryan Coogler, Joe Robert Cole

big stan agario @bigstanagario

FollowFollow @bigstanagario

@Ryan Coogler @theblackpanther Hello, is the model for #BlackPanther#MartinLutherKing and for #Killmonger #MalxomX? I'm more on X side.:-)

#BlackGirlMagic

According to Wilson (2016) in *HuffPost* this hashtag was created by CaShawn Thompson as a way to celebrate the beauty, power and resilience of black women. The goal of this hashtag is to document the many examples of awesome black women around the world. There have been a number of high-profile promotions for #BlackGirlMagic including: *Essence Magazine's* tribute to young black women shaping the future (Wilson, 2018), *CNN*'s look at how the hashtag has encouraged people to affirm the beauty and worth of black women (Thomas, 2016), and Janelle Monae's evening of Black Girl Magic and Love when releasing her new album (Hennemuth, 2018). Selected examples of #BlackGirlMagic tweets include:

Jadian @Jadiand Apr 26

Finishing undergrad while single parenting and dealing with lupus wasn't easy. Went from sleeping in my car to my mom's sofa, dropping out, going back, becoming financially stable and now I'm receiving my BA in Communication. I did it all for you, Jolie. #gradszn **#blackgirlmagic**

Bonang B* Matheba Verified account @bonang_m Apr 22

... she's from Botswana. Her music is amazing. 💜 #MphoSebina **#BlackGirlMagic**

Madré 3000, M.Ed MA-MFT @PushaTease Apr 26

Miracle Hines @MiracleHines_ 15m15 minutes ago

The odds are always stacked up against black women but we somehow brake every tree of doubt and hardship down. There is nothing that can hold us back or down, I'm proud to be a black woman with so much strength and power running through me. #BlackGirlMagic

Tamaria @mestrellabeauty 17m17 minutes ago

Dear Self, Today, You will shine.

Shayna Price @ShaynaTheGreat 25m25 minutes ago

Married, 2 kids, full course load, working nights to secure the bag. They said it couldn't be done. We laughed at them and said ITS ALREADY DONE & WE ARE JUST GETTING STARTED

Rowana Abbensetts @Rowana_A 8h8 hours ago

Not everyone who is **#blackgirlmagic** is also your friend. I'm all for solidarity, but not everyone is wishing you well or wants to see you win.

J.W. @beingpurposeful Apr 23

"The magic of being a black girl is that there is a broad spectrum of black girls from skin tone, to hair type, body type, ability, and many other varying factors unique to each person. Our differences and how we define them in our own way make us magical." #blackgirlmagic

#OscarsSoWhite

The #OscarsSoWhite hashtag was created to address the lack of diversity in award nominations. *The Los Angeles Times* reported that in 2012 the Academy was 94% white and 77% male, and two years later those numbers dropped only slightly to 91% and 76% respectively (Keagan, Poindexter, & Whipp, 2016). This controversial hashtag changed the way the Academy operates and plans were made to double the number of female and minority members by 2020 (Ryan, 2016). April Reign, the managing editor of BroadwayBlack.com was upset by the all-white nominee lists, so she sent the hashtag trending (Anderson, 2016). This hashtag inspired a number of prominent people in the industry to boycott the Oscars ceremony in 2016 including: Spike Lee, Will and Jada Pinkett Smith, and Michael Moore (Filipov & Stapleton, 2016). Selected examples of #OscarsSoWhite tweets include:

Saxton Simmons @simms_saxton Follow @simms_saxton

This lack of diversity within Hollywood is because there are only a few movie companies that will cast people of color for roles. One reason for this could be that people in charge of casting are predominantly white. #OscarsSoWhite 1:25 PM—24 Apr 2018

S Brent Plate @splate1 Follow @splate1

"It's not only that it would be more equitable to have more actors of color on the big screen, it's that having more actors of color might actually change the racist presumptions of our culture at large." #OscarsSoWhite #visualculture http://the-conversation.com/how-images-change-our-race-bias-94368?utm_source=twitter&utm_medium=twitterbutton … @ConversationUS

April ✔@ReignOfApril

A five minute opening by brilliant Chris Rock will not make up for over 80 years of erasure of marginalized communities. #OscarsSoWhite 9:02 AM—Jan 14, 2016

Nation State of Mind @OmowaleAfrika Mar 9

Blk ppl have been conditioned to operate on the notion that we can't love/value ourselves, unless white society does so first. Whether it's Bruno Mars, #Oscarssowhite, or the cry for #Blackrepresentstion. These behaviors are all rooted in our desperate need for white acceptance.

AJ+ Verified account @ajplus Feb 26

"Clueless" star Stacey Dash is running for Congress. The actress filed paperwork to run in California's 44th district. Here's a refresher: -She called the #OscarsSoWhite boycott "ludicrous" -She said there's no need for Black History Month -She was fired from Fox News

#LemonadeSyllabus

Beyonce's "Lemonade" album had a significant impact throughout the interpretive community called Black Twitter. According to *Essence Magazine* (2016), #LemonadeSyllabus brought about female empowerment, black pride, and knowledge. The series was created by Candice Benbow, a Ph.D. student at Princeton Theological Seminary in order to celebrate what it means to be a black woman. Once the request was made Benbow received hundreds of submissions such as, poems, books, music, and articles for the syllabus. The discussion surrounding Beyonce's Lemonade album has been extraordinary. Selected examples of #LemonadeSyllabus tweets include:

Melissa Harris-Perry Verified account @MHarrisPerry

Following @MHarrisPerry I love @CandiceBenbow's #LemonadeSyllabus. http://candicebenbow.com/lemonadesyllabus/ …

Josie Geller @luvleemelodie 9 May 2016

Just printed my **#LemonadeSyllabus**. Ready! Thank you @CandiceBenbow

Women's March Verified account @womensmarch Follow @womensmarch

#Lemonade was released 1 year ago yesterday. #ReflectAndResist with the #LemonadeSyllabus: https://issuu.com/candicebenbow/docs/lemonade_syllabus_2016 … Follow @TwitterMoments

Okay class, now let's get in #Formation for @CandiceBenbow's #LemonadeSyllabus. 🐝 🍋 Nerd out about Beyoncé with the Lemonade syllabus Trending May 9, 2016

Writer and educator Candice Benbow went the academic route to show her love for Beyoncé's new album by asking black women to suggest books, films, and art that would best accompany Lemonade. She then compiled the responses into an e-book called #LemonadeSyllabus.

fowlerbird @fowlerbird 20 Jul 2018

Over 200 resources were compiled by black women ranging from classics to self-care under the hashtag #lemonadesyllabus. https://www.left-bank.com/lemonade-syllabus-reading-list … #STEMLibSouth18

Rebecca Bodenheimer @rmbodenheimer 6 Jun 2018

Rebecca Bodenheimer Retweeted

What @CandiceBenbow went thru is horrendous. Academia is toxic as hell & that goes double for Ivies. I'm sorry you were mistreated & cast aside like this—thank you for speaking up. You were the mastermind behind the #lemonadesyllabus so I know you'll continue to do great things.

#StayMadAbby

In 2016 the U.S. Supreme Court upheld the legality of Affirmative Action in college admissions based on a lawsuit by Abigail Fisher against the University of Texas (Kingkade, 2016). Kingkade explains that Texas seniors in the top 10% of their graduating class can attend any state school. Fisher's grades did not make the cut so she sued. In a four to three decision the Court disagreed and #StayMadAbby surged. Jones (2016) says the lawsuit argued that under the equal protection concept of the 14th Amendment considering race for admissions through Affirmative Action hurts the rights of White Americans. But apparently the courts did not agree. Selected examples of #StayMadAbby include:

Brotha B @BlakeDontCrack Follow @BlakeDontCrack

If Abby did her research she might not have sued because white women are the largest beneficiaries of Affirmative Action. 🐸 🍰

#StayMadAbby **Aggressive Asian** Verified account @JennLi123 Follow @JennLi123

How white ppl think college admission works: black ppl: affirmative action! Asian ppl: Magic DNA! White ppl: We earned it! #StayMadAbby 2:19 PM—23 Jun 2016

Juke Joint Jezebel @MercurialMiss Follow @MercurialMiss

I ALMOST feel sorry for Fisher. She's clearly a dimwitted pawn 4 her lawyers crusade against minorities. #StayMadAbby #BeckyWithTheBadGrades 12:31 PM—23 Jun 2016

Assy @assyme0w Follow @assyme0w

If there ever were a case of a picture being worth a thousand words, this would be it. #WhitePrivilege #StayMadAbby

W. Earl Sparrow Jr. @MrSparrow May 13

Replying to @CharlesMBlow

The people who are "outraged" at #AffirmativeAction should be "outraged" at this scandal. Affirmative action students had to qualify academically. These rich, white kids DIDN'T qualify academically. Where is #StayMadAbby and her ilk? This just proves their rage is racist.

Tracey Verified account @traceylross

FollowFollow @traceylross

When you can't get into the school you want and blame people of color ... only to find out it be your own people.

Chezare A. Warren @DrChezareWarren Mar 14

Perhaps, we should be more understanding of all these wealthy YT ppl stealing elite college admissions. It must suck to know that the systems established to most benefit you, hate you too. The rest of us of a darker hue have held this understanding for a long time. #StayMadAbby

Angelo Guisado @VoltaireLaFlare Follow @VoltaireLaFlare

Donald Trump Jr (somehow admitted to Penn) again proving that LEGACY admissions, not #affirmativeaction, is the real injustice #staymadabby

6:51 PM—10 Jul 2017

#TweetLikeThe1600s and #IfSlaveryWasAChoice

Not all of the popular hashtags on Black Twitter are positive and supported by everyone. #TweetLikeThe1600s created a huge controversy. On February 1, 2018 *The Grio* called the hashtag hilarious and horrible at the same time. According to the article, the purpose of the hashtag was to create hypothetical slavery scenarios (*The Grio*, 2018). In *Hip Hop Wired*, Strong (2018) says the hashtag is all in fun. He maintains that Black Twitter is an unstoppable force when it comes to wit and humor.

Even though he later apologized for saying it, Kanye West triggered another distasteful hashtag #IfSlaveryWasAChoice. In an interview with TMZ West actually said that 400 years of slavery sounds like a choice (Leight, 2018). Selected examples of #TweetLikeThe1600s and #IfSlaveryWasAChoice include:

Son of N'Jobu @OGIndifferent Follow @OGIndifferent

*my MASSA hat is signed (Trump hat) 👑👑👑👑👑👑👑
#tweetlikethe1600s RT @loncho1000: When that first whip hit yo back #tweetlikethe1600s

Flightbae™😊 @justcallmeBABA Follow @justcallmeBABA
The #IfSlaveryWasAChoice has just turned into #tweetlikethe1600s and the tweets are just as distasteful. Particularly considering why this whole thing started, it gives the impression that we never really cared, It's false outrage and it's only okay when WE mock slavery

Rich @therealminter Follow @therealminter Replying to @_TheCivilRight
This reeks of that God awful #Tweetlikethe1600s hashtag. I've never been more embarrassed and disgusted in my people. 3:53 AM—2 May 2018 from Mountain Park, GA

The Social Secret @iamsecretb Follow @iamsecretb
I think #Tweetlikethe1600s and #IfSlaveryWasAChoice are good for the soul. Laughter heals. Kanye is stupid. That is all.

POOPITY SCOOP @joseph__amiel Follow @joseph__amiel
#IfSlaveryWasAChoice Massa: "Are you coming to the field to pick cotton?"
Slave: "Who all there?"

Jamillia Bernard @MilliaJay 19 Dec 2018
Can we bring #Tweetlikethe1600s back please. I need some joy in my life

❤ 🎨Aliya Michelle ❤ 🎨 @MyHeartYourArt 4 May 2018
Wow. Some folks are rationalizing that #SlaveryWasAChoice because slaves could've chosen death over slavery. The GAG is, MANY did DIE!!! Be glad YOUR ancestors didn't choose suicide. Otherwise, you wouldn't be here to post such ignorance. 😒 ASS … HOLE #IfSlaveryWasAChoice

I am Eri'Oluwa @ApostleEriOluwa 13 Jun 2018
Ignorance is bad. Arrogant ignorance is worst. But foolish ignorance is dangerous. These explains why ignorant Kanye West thought #SlaveryWasAChoice If his forefathers had a choice he would be somewhere in Nigeria singing Fuji, or in South Africa singing Kwaito. Give him a History Book

#DonLemonLogic

A number of comments made by *CNN*'s Don Lemon have become controversial Black Twitter trends. Carrasquillo (2013) explains that Lemon said blacks should stop wearing baggy pants and using the N-word. He also suggested that he supported the stop and frisk policy to help stop crime. Of course, Black Twitter lit up. Apparently, many people were not happy with his comments. They criticized him for pushing his own values and judgments about respectability on everyone. Another issue occurred in *The Grio* (2014), when Lemon took issue with being called an

Uncle Tom and said dressing and speaking appropriately are things his mom taught him. Selected examples of #DonLemonLogic and #DonLemonOn include:

Segun Idowu @revrenddoctor

#DonLemonOn Don Lemon: Would you rather be acceptable to whites and get paid to hate yourself or be liked by the coloreds and get nothing? 11:30 AM—Nov 5, 2013

Tracy Boomeisha-Ann Clayton ✔ @brokeymcpoverty

!! RT @BoyNamedTawanda: Don Lemon on Slavery: would you rather be free and unemployed or have a home and a job? 11:24 AM—Nov 5, 2013

Powur Houz @PowurHoose Follow @PowurHoose

#DonLemonLogic As soon as I pulled my pants up I got a scholarship to Harvard, Rush Limbaugh went off the air, and Cops love me now! 10:05 AM—30 Jul 2013

Marc W. Polite @marcpolite Follow @marcpolite

Until black people are perfect, they deserve to be oppressed #DonLemonLogic

PragmaticObotsUnite @PragObots Follow @PragObots

If only blacks would stop littering, Repubs would stop trying to disenfranchise black voters. #DonLemonLogic 12:04 PM—28 Jul 2013

Black Twitter promotes the black agenda in America. It enables a powerful critique of Black experience within mainstream society. The shared notion of blackness is a crucial element when it comes to participation on Black Twitter. Black people are not a monolithic community, but there are histories, commonalities, and understandings that bring black people together as well as separate them. Black Twitter presents key moments in history that highlight vital situations and offer broad accessibility for all who participate.

These participants identify with worthy cultural topics using their access to accumulate cultural capital. Black Twitter as a two-way dialogue is also critical to the process of creating culturally resonant connections. Social and culture meaning is debated and defined through public engagement with Black Twitter as a key force of interconnectedness.

Large mainstream news organizations on numerous occasions have had to change their reporting or shift the focus of a story because of prominent Black Twitter trends. Pitner (2015) believes that most white people should read Black Twitter to better understand what matters to black people. He talks about the shift in appreciation by the *Los Angeles Times* which has actually hired a full-time reporter to cover Black Twitter and other social media feeds.

> For the uninitiated, Black Twitter isn't some organized effort. There is no central organizing apparatus of Black Twitter that is coordinating hashtags. There is no mission statement, and there is no clearly defined purpose. It is simply Black Americans

talking to one another about what matters most to them. But what makes it new is that all of this is occurring within an environment where non-black voices can overhear the conversations.

As part of her study on Black Twitter, Clark (2014) splits the site into three levels of connection; personal community, thematic notions, and meta-network (Ramsey, 2015). First, personal community encompasses the connections made. Second, thematic notes involves the subject matter and satisfies the need for information. Third, meta-network is how the personal community and thematic notions link creating a critical conversation. Clark (2014) believes the creation of a hashtag is influential because it motivates participants to support or resist certain topics building cultural competency and amassing cultural capital.

Dominant media are finally starting to better understand the power of race and social media, specifically when they see the significance of Black Twitter participants engaging in social, cultural, and political communication. Black Twitter as an interpretive community represents and regulates cultural wealth for those who use it as a resource for influence, knowledge and control.

References

Aden, R. C., Rahoi, R. L., & Beck, C. (1995). Dreams are born on places like this: The process of interpretive community formation at the *Field of Dreams* site. *Communication Quarterly, 43*(4), 368–380.

Anderson, T. (2016, January 14). #OscarsSoWhite creator on Oscar noms: 'Don't tell me that people of color, women cannot fill seats'. *The Los Angeles Times*. Retrieved from https://www.latimes.com/entertainment/envelope/la-et-mn-april-reign-oscars-so-white-diversity-20160114-story.html

Baldridge, B. (2014). Relocating the deficit: Reimagining black youth in neoliberal times. *American Research Journal, 51*(3), 440–472.

Beck, C. S. (1995). You make the call: The co-creation of media text through interaction in an interpretive community of Giant fans. *The Electronic Journal of Communication, 5*(1).

Berkowitz, D., & TerKeurst, J. (1999, September). Community as interpretive community: Rethinking the journalist source relationship. *Journal of Communication, 49*(3), 125–136.

Bourdieu, P., & Passerson, J. C. (1979). *The Inheritors, French students and their relation to culture.* Chicago, IL: University of Chicago Press.

Brock, A. (2012). From the blackhand side: Twitter as a cultural conversation. *Journal of Broadcasting and Electronic Media, 56*(4), 529–549.

Byrd, W. C., Gilbert, K. L., & Richardson Jr., J. B. (2017). The vitality of social media for establishing a research agenda on black lives and the movement. *Ethnic and Racial Studies, 4*(11), 1872–1881.

Carrasquillo, A. (2013, July 28). *CNN's* Don Lemon under fire after he says blacks shouldn't wear baggy pants, use n-word. *Litter*. Retrieved from https://www.buzzfeed.com/adrian-carrasquillo/cnns-don-lemon-under-fire-after-he-says-blacks-shouldnt-wear?utm_term=.ql6JEQME8#.dn5EJbBJV

Clark, M. (2014). To tweet our own cause: A mixed-methods study of the online phenomenon "Black Twitter." *ProQuest Dissertations*.

Coyle K., & Lindlof, T. (1988, May). *Exploring the universe of science fiction: Interpretive communities and readers genres*. Paper presented at the International Communication Conference, New Orleans.

Dixon, J. (2011). Social media plays greater role in cause engagement for African Americans and Hispanics. *Dynamics of Cause Engagement*. Washington, DC: Georgetown University Center for Social Impact Communication.

Essence.com. (2016, April 29). #LemonadeSyllabus: Black women are sharing reading lists inspired by Beyonce's visual album and it's amazing. Retrieved from https://www.essence.com/news/lemonadesyllabus-black-women-sharing-reading-lists-beyonce-album/

Filipov, D., & Stapleton, J. P. (2016, February 29). Oscars race controversy spurs protests, parodies. *Boston Globe*. Retrieved from https://www.bostonglobe.com/arts/movies/2016/02/28/oscars-race-controversy-spurs-protests parodies/ Vk9ckOdlXWpEWrOzlXc4TP/story.html

Fish, S. (1980). *Is there a text in this class? The authority of interpretive communities*. Cambridge, MA: Harvard University Press.

Fox, S., Zickuhr, K., & Smith, A. (2009). Twitter and status updating. *Pew Internet and the American Life Project*. Retrieved from http://pewinternet.org/Reports/2009/17-Twitter-and-status-updating.aspx.

Franklin, V. P. (2002). Introduction: cultural capital and African American education. The *Journal of African American History, 87*, 175–181.

Gray, H. (1989). *Watching race: Television and the struggle for blackness*. Minneapolis: University of Minnesota.

The Grio. (2014, October 28). Don Lemon says he's called an "Uncle Tom" a lot. Retrieved from https://thegrio.com/2014/10/28/don-lemon-uncle-tom-cnn/

The Grio. (2018, February 1). 'TweetLikeThe1600s' hashtag mocking slavery is hilarious and horrible at the same time. Retrieved from https://thegrio.com/2018/02/01/tweet-like-the-1600s-black-twitter/

Harlow, S., & Benbrook A. (2017, October 10). How #Blacklivesmatters: Exploring the rle of hip hop celebrities in constructing racial identity on Black Twitter. *Information Communication and Society, 22*(3), 352–368.

Hennemuth, B. (2018, April 27). Jonelle Monae celebrates her new album with an evening of black girl magic and love. *Vanity Fair*. Retrieved from https://www.vanityfair.com/style/2018/04/janelle-monae-dirty-computer-party

Hill, J. H. (1995). Language, race, and white public space. *American Anthropologist, 100*(3), 680–689.

Hill, M. L. (2018). "Thank you, Black Twitter": State violence, digital counterpublics, and pedagogies of resistance. *Urban Education, 53*(2), 286–302.

Holub, C. (2018, March 20). *Black Panther* is the most tweeted about movie of all time. *Entertainment Weekly*. Retrieved from http://ew.com/movies/ 2018/03/ 20/black-panther-most-tweeted-movie-all-time/

Hymes, D. H. (1980). *Language in education* (pp. 1–18). Washington, DC: Center for Applied Linguistics.

Ince, J., Rojas, F., & Davis, C. A. (2017). The social media response to Black Lives Matter: How Twitter users interact with Black Lives Matter through hashtag use. *Ethnic and Racial Studies, 40*(11), 1814–1830.

Jensen, K. B. (1990). Television futures: A social action methodology for studying interpretive communities. *Critical Studies in Mass Communication, 7*(2), 1–18.

Jensen, K. B. (1991). When is meaning? Communication theory, pragmatism, and mass media reception. *Communication Yearbook, 14*, 3–31. Newbury Park, CA: Sage.

Jones, N. H. (2016, June 23). What Abigail Fisher's Affirmative Action case was really about. *ProPublica*. Retrieved from https://www.propublica.org/article/a-colorblind-constitution-what-abigail-fishers-affirmative-action-case-is-r

Keagan, R., Poindexter, S., & Whipp, G. (2016, February 26). 91% white, 76% male: Changing who votes on the Oscars won't be easy. *The Los Angeles Times*. Retrieved from http://graphics.latimes.com/oscars-2016-voters/

Kingkade, T. (2016, June 23). #StayMadAbby makes triumphant return after Supreme Court Affirmative Action ruling. *HuffPost*. Retrieved from https://www.huffingtonpost.com/entry/ staymadabby-affirmative-action_us_576bf911e4b0795798cb464e

Leight, E. (2018, May 1). Kanye says 400 years of slaver 'sounds like a choice'. *Rolling Stone*. Retrieved from https://www.rollingstone.com/music/music-news/kanye-west-says-400-years-of-slavery-sounds-like-a-choice-628849/

Liebes, T., & Katz, E. (1990). Interactions with "Dallas": Cross cultural readings of American TV. *Canadian Journal of Communication, 15*(1), 45–66.

McDaniels, S. (2017). Twitter and the #BlackLivesMatter movement. *ProQuest Dissertations*.

Mitchell, T. (2005). An African American religious interpretive community's reception of the electronic church via a para-social interaction investigation. *ProQuest Dissertations*.

Mone, B. (2017, August 15). Beyond Black Twitter: A social media community uncovered. *Medium.com*. Retrieved from https://medium.com/@CestLaBrianna/beyond-blacktwitter-a-social-media-community-uncovered-74812df189a8

Pitner, B. H. (2015, July 18). White people should read Black Twitter. *The Daily Beast*. Retrieved from https://www.thedailybeast.com/white-people-should-read-black-twitter

Radway, J. (1984). *Reading the romance: Women, patriarchy and popular literature.* Chapel Hill: University of North Carolina Press.

Ramsey, D. (2015, April 10). The truth about Black Twitter. *The Atlantic.* Retrieved from https://www.theatlantic.com/technology/archive/2015/04/the-truth-about-black-twitter/390120/

Ray, R., Brown, M., & Laybourn, W. (2017). The evolution of #BlackLivesMatter on Twitter: social movements, big data, and race. *Ethnic and Racial Studies, 40*(11), 1795–1796.

Ray, R., Brown, M., Fraistat, N., & Summers, E. (2017). Ferguson and the death of Michael Brown on Twitter: #BlackLivesMatter, #TCOT, and the evolution of collective identities. *Ethnic and Racial Studies, 40*(11), 1797–1813.

Ryan, P. (2016, February 22). #OscarSoWhite controversy, what you need to know. *USA Today.* Retrieved from https://www.usatoday.com/story/life/movies/2016/02/02/oscars-academy-award-nominations-diversity/79645542/

Schroder, K. C. (1994). Audience semiotics, interpretive communities and the "ethnographic turn". *Media Research. Media, Culture and Society, 16,* 337–347.

Smith, J. (2018, February 11). The revolutionary power of *Black Panther. Time.com.* Retrieved from http://time.com/black-panther/

Strong, L. (2018, January 31). Black Twitter has #TweetLikeThe1600s trending topic going crazy. *Hip Hop Wired.* Retrieved from http://hiphopwired.com/743101/black-twitter-has-tweetlikethe1600s-trending-topic-going-crazy/

Taylor, K. (2016). *From #BlackLivesMatter to black liberation.* Chicago, IL. Haymarket Books.

Thomas, J. (2016, February 24). Black Girl Magic is more than a hashtag, it's a movement. *CNN.* Retrieved from https://www.cnn.com/2016/02/24/living/black-girl-magic-feat/index.html

Wilson, J. (2016, January 12). The meaning of #BlackGirlMagic, and how you can get some of it. *HuffPost.* Retrieved from https://www.huffingtonpost.com/entry/what-is-black-girl-magic-video_us_5694dad4e4b086bc1cd517f4

Wilson, A. (2018, December 4) The biggest black girl magic moments we lived for in 2018. BlackGirlMagic *Essence Magazine.* Retrieved from https://www.essence.com/culture/the-biggest-black-girl-magic-moments-we-lived-for-in-2018/

Yosso, T. J. (2005, March). Whose culture has capital? A Critical Race Theory discussion of community cultural wealth. *Race, Ethnicity and Education, 8*(1), 69–91.

Zelizer, B. (1993). Journalists as interpretive communities. *Critical Studies in Media Communication, 10*(3), 219–237.

CHAPTER NINE

President Barack Obama: Biased Frames and Microaggressions

Barack Obama became the forty-fourth president of the United States of America on January 20, 2009 (Hulse, 2009). He was the first black president in the history of the country. Joseph (2017) believes that having a black president for eight years changed America forever.

> The presence of the Obamas on the world stage confirmed deep seeded truths about black excellence, love and humanity that we've always taken for granted despite white denial of these very truths. ... they broke powerful barriers installed by the nation's brutal history of slavery, Jim Crow and institutional racism.

The changes in society that led to the election of a black president have been enhanced by the browning of America. Klein (2018) believes that this is one reason why the election of a black president was so polarizing and the unity of a young, multiracial coalition created by the occasion also seemed stark and threatening to some. Although issues surrounding race were discussed less by President Obama while in office than by any other president since Franklin Roosevelt, race was still a relevant dynamic throughout his presidency according to Klein.

> "Obama's presidency didn't force race to the forefront of American politics through rhetoric or action but through symbolism. Obama himself was a symbol of a changing

America, of White America's loss of power, of the fact that the country was changing and new groups were gaining power."

Klein (2018) also includes examples from popular talk show hosts as confirmation. For example, Rush Limbaugh and Bill O'Reilly were good illustrations of the white fear that was constantly propagandized. Limbaugh told his listeners, "How do you get promoted in the Barack Obama administration? By hating white people ... making white people the new minority." O'Reilly claimed, "It's not a traditional America anymore. They are fifty-percent of the voting public who want stuff. And who is going to give them things? President Obama ... the white establishment is now the minority."

According to Colby and Ortman (2015) the demographics of this country are changing and that is a difficult situation for some to accept. When looking at projections of births, deaths, and immigration in the Census Bureau data they found that the non-Hispanic white population is currently the majority with more than a fifty percent share of the total population, but by 2060 that group will drop to just forty-four percent. While they will still remain the largest group, Asians, Hispanics and blacks are expected to grow at a faster rate and combined those groups will create a majority minority America (Colby & Ortman, 2015).

The politics of resentment was a consistent frame used by the Republican party during Obama's tenure. This included a variety of concerns such as the downsizing and outsourcing of jobs, immigration others, and Affirmative Action linked to the "us versus them" mentality. The politics of resentment is a biased racial frame that drives people to the negative side of things. Before he became president, Obama dismissed the polemic that was building between people. In his book *The Audacity of Hope* (2006) he explained that the most important way to help white workers was also to help black and brown workers.

> These days, what ails working-class and middle-class blacks and Latinos is not fundamentally different than what ails their white counterparts: downsizing, outsourcing, automation, wage stagnation, the dismantling of employer based healthcare and pension plans, and schools that fail to teach young people the skills they need to compete in a global economy ... and what would help minority workers are the same things that would help white workers. (p. 245)

Biased Frames and Microaggressions

For this exemplar Entman's (2007) redesign concerning the notion of bias as a conceptual umbrella is used. It includes the concepts of agenda setting, framing, and priming. According to Entman, framing boosts the salience of ideas along with agenda setting and it also influences perceptions, interpretations and preferences through priming. He adds, "[framing is] the process of culling a few elements of perceived reality and assembling a narrative that highlights connections among them to promote a particular interpretation" (p. 164).

Biased framing was involved when it came to many images and messages concerning the first Black American President. Relevant patterns of racial bias can be found in a variety of mediated texts. Entman's model can specifically demonstrate how agenda setting, framing and priming in the media were used to promote the cultural difference of Barack Obama. And how that cultural difference ultimately became a constant challenge to his credibility as the first black president in the United States.

It is crucial to note that politics is one area where racism is alive and well. In fact, while the other areas of racialism: stereotypes, biased frames, and historical myths also function in political realms racism is strongest because of the direct link to power. The stereotypes, biased frames, and historical myths that are perpetuated in the political arena can be used to influence real policies that impact black communities disproportionately ultimately creating racism. Reed (2010) in his book *Barack Obama and the Jim Crow Media* critiques a number of the attacks on President Obama as racist. Reed says the term "nigger breakers" is used by Fredrick Douglass in his autobiography when describing how slaves were beaten until they broke. He compares that term to the oppositional politicians and media pundents who kept up a constant barrage of confrontations and insults aimed at breaking the first black president.

According to Huber and Solorzano (2015) racial microaggressions are based on consistent everyday assaults. There are many examples of racial microaggressions that were experienced by President Obama through verbal and nonverbal attacks, layered confrontations, and cumulative incursions. Pierce (1970) describes racial microaggressions as "offensive mechanisms" sometimes subtle, sometimes stunning.

Lakoff (2006) discusses the notion of macroaggressions as the larger ideological foundation embedded in normalized racial practices. He says macroaggressions are:

> The set of beliefs and/or ideologies that justify actual or potential social arrangements that legitimate the interests and/or positions of a dominant group over non-dominant groups, that in turn leads to related structures and acts of subordination.

During routine moments, racial micro and macroaggressions often become part of the everyday experience. They include visual images, language, behaviors, and various problematic interactions. They can be conscious or unconscious, systematic or random. Gee (2001) examined how discourse is used to perpetuate micro and macro aggressions defining discourse as a process that involves socialization based on how an audience consumes, interprets, and learns from the text.

Political Examples

Unfortunately, the successful 2008 and 2012 election campaigns, plus the two terms served by the first black president in the United States, brought to the forefront numerous waves of biased framing, microaggressions, macroaggressions and racism. From Republican representative Joe Wilson's "You lie" outburst during President Obama's address to Congress and the constant beat of the birther movement to social media images of watermelon patches outside the White House and the iconic image of Jan Brewer the former Arizona governor pointing her finger in President Obama's face, he could not escape connections to his race no matter how hard he tried. And he did try.

During the 2008 campaign, it was obvious that Obama wanted to keep the issue of race at a distance. The last thing he needed was for a majority of White Americans to see him as a stereotypical black man. He stayed away from stereotypes like angry, aggressive, and threatening only to be labeled soft, a pushover, and weak based on his calm and appeasing nature. At one point he was actually called "no drama Obama" and it was not seen as a positive marker (Rogers, 2014).

Because they could not pin the aggressive black man stereotype on Obama, his pastor Reverend Jeremiah Wright was targeted. Through agenda setting, some in the media used Wright to argue that Obama must be racist since Wright was his minister and Wright had made racist comments in the pulpit. A few negative segments from several sermons over a thirty-year career were pulled out and played in a repetitive media loop until he was forced to address the controversy. It was in response to the media's push to frame him in a cloud of black hatred that Obama delivered his 2008 race speech and became the perfect example of a powerful, yet caring black man.

In the 2008 race speech, Obama admitted that Reverend Wright's words were not only wrong but they were divisive at a time when unity was needed. He went on to describe his former pastor as encompassing both good and bad traits (National Constitutional Center, 2008; Obama, 2008). He also explained the broader context that was tied to Reverend Wright's anger such as slavery, inequality, discrimination, and racism. Finally, he offered a simple comparison priming the audience to think and feel differently about the issue.

> I could no more disown him [Rev. Wright] than I can disown the black community. I can no more disown him than I can my white grandmother, a woman who helped raise me, a woman who sacrificed again and again for me, a woman who loves me as much as she loves anything else in this world, but a woman who once confessed her fear of black men who passed her on the street and who on more than one occasion has uttered racial or ethnic stereotypes that made me cringe. These people are a part of me. And they are a part of America, this country that I love.

Throughout both campaigns and both presidential terms, Barack Obama felt the racist rumblings of the birther issue. The initiation of this lie has been traced back to 2004 when Alan Keyes during an Illinois U.S. Senate race claimed that Obama wasn't a "true Christian" (Gore, 2017). In that same year, another Illinois political candidate Andy Martin suggested that Obama could be a closet Muslim because of his name (Cheney, 2016).

Donald Trump pushed the lie as far as he could calling for President Obama to release his birth certificate. But despite the Hawaii Department of Health releasing Obama's short-form birth certificate in 2008 the conspiracy theory continued to thrive (Daily Kos, 2008). The birther issue was framed shamefully as propagandist hate concerning cultural difference in order to take away support from the first black president in America.

Other right-wing Republicans attached themselves to the birther issue and added more lies. Certain racial images and messages were defined as worthy of public attention (Hughey & Parks, 2014). For example, more than 17 million people viewed a video on YouTube that falsely declared, "Obama Admits He's a Muslim." Gore (2017), however, reported that the video conversation had been edited in two specific places. First, the spot where Obama said he was a Christian was removed and second those places where he said he had Muslim relatives or had lived in Muslim countries were twisted in a way to suggest that he was claiming to be a Muslim instead.

Various fake emails and news stories were also created to influence audience interpretations in a negative way. For example, viral emails lied about Obama using a *Koran* for his swearing in ceremony rather than a *Bible*. A fake *Associated Press* story accused Obama of receiving a Fulbright scholarship for foreign students at Occidental College, but it was quickly proven false (Kiely, 2016). Finally, a derogatory connection to Affirmative Action was formed when Trump and others implied that he could not have possibly gotten into Columbia or Harvard based on his own merits. An article in *Jack and Jill Politics* called these types of biased frames "savvy racism" because Affirmative Action represents a source of resentment for both conservatives and liberals (Melber, 2011).

Although some media pundits called the flow of conspiracy theories "Hysteria," others continued to plug away (Page, 2017). Right wing talk show host Rush Limbaugh consistently primed his listeners with falsehoods claiming Obama was un-American, a foreigner, and also questioning the Hawaiian birth certificate (Dyson, 2016). Limbaugh's promotion of a song called "Barack the Magic Negro" started even more controversy. According to Barker (2008), the song was written by Paul Shanklin and based on the melody from "Puff the Magic Dragon." The lyrics suggested that supporting a black man like Barack made guilty white people feel good and pointed out that he was not authentically black or from the hood. The song ended with an inverse insult (within black culture) that said Obama was articulate and bright.

Donald Trump revived the birther lie during the 2011 presidential campaign calling President Obama's short-form birth certificate a fraud. Trump then lied again. He said he had people look into Obama's background and they couldn't believe what they found, when ultimately, they found nothing (Krieg, 2016). Even when Obama's long-form birth certificate was released in April of 2011, Trump did not let it rest (Daily, Kos, Lopez, 2017).

As the first Black American president, race was the focus of a number of biased frames and microaggressions. For example, in the political arena the color of Obama's skin, along with the foreign sound of his name fueled already existing perceptions of racial and cultural difference. This difference brought forth criticisms about his leadership ability, integrity, intelligence, and experience. For some Obama was too black and for others he was not black enough (Adesioye, 2008).

The July 2008 cover of *The New Yorker Magazine* (Blitt, 2008) presented a sketch of Barack and Michelle Obama framing them as terrorists sharing a fist bump. Barack was dressed in a Muslim thobe and turban while his wife flaunted a large afro, carried an AK-47, and wore combat boots. They were standing in the oval office where a large portrait of Osama Bin Laden hung over the fireplace and an American flag burned inside the fireplace. In an *NPR* interview, the editor of the magazine called it satire and claimed they were poking fun at the "politics of fear" (NPR, 2008). But for many Americans this image did not register as satire at all, instead it solidified a problematic conspiracy theory that Obama might be a secret Muslim.

Despite the fact that the *New Yorker* cover was apparently meant to be satire, that cover confirmed that the black presidential candidate and his wife were outsiders. It suggested that they did not fit in, his name Barack Hussein Obama had an obvious connection to Arab and Muslim culture, and the question of his birthplace was still an issue (Allen, 2008). Obama's presidency became a battle as his presidential potential was layered with ethnic discrepancies where cultural, political, and psychological lies were constructed through biased racial framing.

It was evident that *FOX* News pundits primed their audience to consider Barack and Michelle Obama in offensive ways. One show described the First Lady as "Obama's baby mama," the fist bump between Barack and Michelle during the Democratic primary was labelled a "terrorist fist jab," and a number of pundits insinuated that Barack hated white people, and he wanted to settle the score with reparations (Huppke, 2018). In a *Newsweek* interview, Obama admitted that if he watched *FOX* news all day long he probably wouldn't vote for himself (Glum, 2017).

An obvious exemplar in a *Fox News* article (2011) involved President Obama's 50th birthday party at the White House. The headline, a racial microaggression read: Obama's Hip Hop BBQ Didn't Create Jobs. There were photos underneath the headline of four black men who attended the event but only one was connected to Hip Hop. The photos included an athlete Charles Barkley, President Obama, a comedian Chris Rock and a rapper Jay Z.

In 2018 *Ranker* offered a number of examples on just how prominent the biased framing surrounding president Obama was on *FOX* news. For example, using comparisons of the first black president with his predecessor they demonstrated how President Obama said he would be open to a meeting with North Korea and it was called "bowing and scraping to dictators" on *FOX*, but President Trump's North Korean love affair with Kim Jong-un was praised and they said, "He should be given credit for trying to make the world a little safer." President Obama's brief time spent on the golf course was called trivial pursuits that took him away from the important things going on in the world, while President Trump enjoyed more than 90 weekend golf outings to resorts that he owned during his first year in office costing the American people one million dollars a day. "Executive order tyranny" was the label for President Obama's actions when he used executive orders to get things done, but when President Trump used executive orders it was seen as simply taking care of his campaign promises. Finally, President Obama's limited political experience was questioned throughout his campaign, yet *FOX* viewers were told that President Trump's lack of political experience was okay and not a cause for concern (Things, 2018).

Unfortunately, biased framing was consistently used to divert attention away from where it should have been during Obama's presidency such as securing important policies like healthcare for all and fulfilling U.S. domestic needs. In a number of cases institutional politics, along with social and economic concerns were automatically tied to negative discourses about race and ethnicity. The best example is Obamacare which became a signature policy for President Obama.

Tired of all the negative rhetoric concerning Obamacare he eventually responded back to the pundits in 2011, "That's right I care" (Jouet, 2014). Obamacare immediately took on a negative connotation about giving poor people, especially people of color free healthcare. At the same time, the actual policy called the Affordable Care Act (ACA) was seen by most Americans as a good thing because everyone deserves decent healthcare (Bacon, 2017).

Waldman (2014) explained that the conservative media primed its audience through warnings that President Obama planned to take revenge on innocent white people for their past sins against blacks. He suggested that every policy President Obama proposed was attached to, "an act of racial vengeance exacted upon whites for the benefit of blacks." The racial divide became so extreme that the average American on the news would argue that Obamacare should be repealed, and at the same time say we should fight for the Affordable Care Act (ACA) because they did not understand that they were the same thing.

On *All Things Considered* (Dropp, 2017), The Chief Research Officer for Morning Consult discussed a survey of 2000 people across the country where 35% did not know that

Obamacare and the Affordable Care Act (ACA) were the same policy. The term Obamacare immediately polarized participants and most did not understand how repealing the Affordable Care Act (ACA) would impact them adversely. Also, a 2015 report by the U.S. Department of Health and Human Services showed that more whites had received insurance coverage under Obamacare than blacks and Latinos combined (Sneed, 2015). In fact, Sneed found that between 2013 and 2015, 7.4 million White Americans received coverage, 4 million Hispanics and 2.6 Black Americans (Dropp & Nyhan, 2017).

Dyson (2016) argued that during Obama's time in office many supporters failed to read the anti-Obama signs and social media outbursts as symptoms of the persistent swirling racist currents in American society.

> As Obama nears the end of his presidency, it's now clear his response to these racist haters was both admirable and flawed. He insisted on celebrating advancements for African-Americans like him, but in so doing delayed the acknowledgment of what was festering: a revived siege of race hate that would sweep the country.

And sweep the country it did once Donald Trump, a reality show huckster, was elected president of the United States instead of Hillary Clinton. While spewing distrust and hatred against difference, Trump vowed to make America great again a message that white supremacists and most people of color knew meant "make America white again" (Delk, 2018; Robinson, 2018; Schwartz, 2018). The biased racial framing that was perpetuated over eight years during President Barack Obama's time in office became even more offensive and insulting under the Trump administration. Simon and Sidner (2018), called America's current agenda under Trump a "state of hate."

Despite the climate afterward, nothing can take away President Obama's election which lifted up a majority of our nation. A black man as president of the United States was scary for white supremacists and the racially ignorant. A daunting future for those who nurture hate can be tied to the projected Census population statistics (Frey, 2018). According to a 2017 report from the Southern Poverty Law Center, Neo-Nazi groups are thriving across the country under the Trump administration (Beirish & Buchanan, 2018). Eight years of hope and change with the first Black American president brought forth a sad period of unapologetic hate, biased framing, unprecedented racial microaggressions, and racism.

References

Adesioye, L. (2008, June 27). Ralph Nader's guilt complex. *The Guardian*. Retrieved from https://www.theguardian.com/commentisfree/2008/jun/27/barackobama.ralphnader

Allen, M. (2008, July 13). Obama slams New Yorker portrayal. *Politico.com*. Retrieved from https://www.politico.com/story/2008/07/obama-slams-new-yorker-portrayal-011719

Bacon Jr., P. (2017, March 23). The Obamacare fight is about way more than healthcare. *FiveThirtyEight*. Retrieved from https://fivethirtyeight.com/features/the-obamacare-fight-is-about-way-more-than-health-care/

Barker, T. (2008, December 30). Barack the magic negro? *The Hill*. Retrieved from https://thehill.com/blogs/pundits-blog/the-administration/31559-barack-the-magic-negro

Beirish, H., & Buchanan, S. (2018, February 11). 2017: The year in hate and extremism. *Southern Poverty Law Center*. Retrieved from https://www.splcenter.org/fighting-hate/intelligence-report/2018/2017-year-hate-and-extremism

Blitt, B. (2008, July 28). The politics of fear cover. *The New Yorker*. Retrieved from https://www.newyorker.com/magazine/2008/07/21

Cheney, K. (2016, September 19). No Clinton didn't start the birther thing. This guy did. *Politico.com*. Retrieved from https://www.politico.com/story/2016/09/birther-movement-founder-trump-clinton-228304

Colby, S., & Ortman, J. (2015, March). Projections of the size and composition of the U.S. population: 2014–2060. *U.S. Census Bureau*. Retrieved from https://www.census.gov/content/dam/Census/library/publications/2015/demo/p25-1143.pdf

Daily Kos. (2008, June 12). Obama's birth certificate. *Daily Kos*. Retrieved from https://www.dailykos.com/stories/2008/6/12/534616/

Delk, J. (2018, January 11). Congressional Black Caucus chairman: Trump's slogan code 'make America white again. *The Hill*. Retrieved from https://thehill.com/blogs/blog-briefing-room/368644-congressional-black-caucus-chairman-trump-slogan-code-for-make

Dropp, K. (2017, February 11). Obamacare and the Affordable Care Act are the same, but Americans still don't know that. *All Things Considered, NPR*. Retrieved from https://www.npr.org/2017/02/11/514732211/obamacare-and-affordable-care-act-are-the-same-but-americans-still-dont-know-that

Dropp, K., & Hyhan, B. (2017, February 7). One-third don't know that Obamacare and the Affordable Care Act are the same. *The New York Times*. Retrieved from https://www.nytimes.com/2017/02/07/upshot/one-third-dont-know-obamacare-and-affordable-care-act-are-the-same.html

Dyson, M. E. (2016, January/February). Whose president was he. *Politico Magazine*. Retrieved from https://www.politico.com/magazine/story/2016/01/barack-obama-race-relations-213493

Entman, R. (2007). Framing bias: Media in the distribution of power. *Journal of Communication*, 57, 163–173.

FOX News's long history of race baiting. (2011, June 13). *Media Matters*. Retrieved from https://www.mediamatters.org/research/2011/06/13/updated-fox-news-

Frey, W. (2018, March 14). The U.S. will become minority white in 2045, Census projects. *Brookings*. Retrieved from https://www.brookings.edu/blog/the-avenue/2018/03/14/the-us-will-become-minority-white-in-2045-census-projects/

Gee, J. P. (2001). Reading as situated language: A social cognitive perspective. *Journal of Adolescent and Adult Literacy*, 44, 714–725.

Glum, J. (2017, December 1). Barack Obama says 'I wouldn't vote for me' if he watched FOX News' weird coverage. *Newsweek*. Retrieved from https://www.newsweek.com/obama-wouldnt-vote-himself-fox-news-728177

Gore, D. (2017, January 19). Eight years of trolling Obama. *Factcheck.org*. Retrieved from https://www.factcheck.org/2017/01/eight-years-of-trolling-obama/

Huber, L. P., & Solorzano, D. G. (2014). Racial microaggressions as a tool for critical race research. Race, *Ethnicity and Education*, 1–23.

Huber, L. P., & Solorzano, D. G. (2015). Visualizing everyday racism: Critical race theory, visual microaggressions, and the historical image of Mexican banditry. *Qualitative Inquiry*, 21(3), 223–238.

Hughey, M., & Parks, G. (2014). *The wrongs of the right: Language, race and the Republican Party in the age of Obama*. New York: New York University Press.

Hulse, C. (2009, January 20). Obama is sworn in as the 44th president. *The New York Times*. Retrieved from https://www.nytimes.com/2009/01/21/us/politics/20web-inaug2.html

Huppke, R. (2018, September 1). When outsiders look in on Black America. *Chicago Tribune*. Retrieved from http://www.chicagotribune.com/news/opinion/chi-obama-race-perspective-story.html#

Joseph, P. (2017, January 7). Barack Obama forever change Black America. *The Guardian*. Retrieved from https://www.theguardian.com/commentisfree/2017/jan/07/barack-obama-forever-changed-black-america

Jouet, M. (2014, January 23). Don't call it Obamacare. *Huffpost*. Retrieved from https://www.huffingtonpost.com/mugambi-jouet/dont-call-the-law-obamaca_b_4116385.html

Kiely, E. (2016, September 19). Trump surrogates spin birther narrative. *Factcheck.org*. Retrieved from https://www.factcheck.org/2016/09/trump-surrogates-spin-birther-narrative/birther-narrative/

Klein, E. (2018, July 30). White threat in a browning America. *Vox*. Retrieved from https://www.vox.com/policy-and-politics/2018/7/30/17505406/trump-obama-race-politics-immigration

Krieg, G. (2016, September 16). 14 of Trump's outrageous birther claims. *CNN*. Retrieved from https://www.cnn.com/2016/09/09/politics/donald-trump-birther/index.html

Lakoff, G. (2006). *Thinking points: Communicating our American values and vision*. New York, NY: Farrar, Straus & Giroux.

Lopez, G. (2017, November 29). Trump is still reportedly pushing his racist birther conspiracy theory about Obama. *Vox.com*. Retrieved from https://www.vox.com/policy-and-politics/2017/11/29/16713664/trump-obama-birth-certificate

McCarter, J. (2011, April 27). Obama releases long form birth certificate. *Daily Kos*. Retrieved from https://www.dailykos.com/stories/2011/4/27/970584/-

Melber, A. (2011, April 27). The Nation: Confronting Trump's coded racism. *NPR Radio*. Retrieved from https://www.npr.org/2011/04/27/135777342/the-nation-confronting-trumps-coded-racism

National Constitutional Center. (2008, March 18). *A more perfect union speech*. Retrieved from https://constitutioncenter.org/amoreperfectunion/

NPR: All Things Considered. (2008, July 14). New Yorker editor defends Obama cover. *NPR*. Retrieved from https://www.npr.org/templates/story/story.php?storyId=92529393

Obama, B. (2006). *The audacity of hope*. New York, NY: Random House.

Obama, B. (2008, March 18). Transcript: Barack Obama's speech on race. *NPR*. Retrieved from https://www.npr.org/templates/story/story.php?storyId=88478467

Page, C. (2017, October 13). The Obama conspiracy theories just keep on coming. *Chicago Tribune*. Retrieved from: https://www.chicagotribune.com/columns/clarence-page/ct-per-spec-page-obama-conspiracy-theories-20171013-story.html

Pierce, C. (1970). Offensive mechanisms. In F. Barbour (Ed.), *The black seventies* (pp. 265–282). Boston: MA: Porter Sargent.

Reed, I. (2010). *Barack Obama and the Jim Crow Media*. Montreal, Canada: Baracka Books

Robinson, E. (2018, July 5). Trump can't make America white again. *The Washington Post*. Retrieved from https://www.washingtonpost.com/opinions/try-as-he-might-trump-cant-make-america-white-again/2018/07/05/0634e02e-8088-11e8-b0effffcabeff946_story.html?utm_term=.bafc84b26e08

Rogers, E. (2014, January 13). The Insiders: The problem with 'no-drama Obama'. *The Washington Post*. Retrieved from https://www.washingtonpost.com/blogs/post-partisan/wp/2014/01/13/the-insiders-the-problem-with-no-drama-obama/?noredirect=on&utm_term=.59e9588c2d54

Schwartz, I. (2018, January 27). Pelosi: Trump immigration plan a campaign to "make America white again." *Real Clear Politics*. Retrieved from https://www.realclearpolitics.com/video/2018/01/27/pelosi_trump_immigration_plan_a_campaign_to_make_america_white_again.html

Simon, M., & Sidner, S. (2018, November 28). In 2008 there was hope. In 2018 there is hurt. This is America's state of hate. *CNN*. Retrieved from https://www.cnn.com/2018/11/26/us/america-state-of-hate/index.html

Sneed, T. (2015, September 22). More whites gain Obamacare coverage than blacks and Latinos combined. *talkingpointsmemo*. Retrieved from https://talkingpointsmemo.com/dc/obamacare-white-black-hispanic-numbers

Things Fox News criticized Obama for but defends Trump for. (2018, June 20). *Ranker*. Retrieved from https://www.ranker.com/list/ways-fox-news-criticized-obama-praises-trump/ranker-news

Waldman, P. (2014, May 23). Yes, opposition to Obamacare is tied up with race. *The Washington Post*. Retrieved from https://www.washingtonpost.com/blogs/plum-line/wp/2014/05/23/yes-opposition-to-obamacare-is-tied-up-with-race/?utm_term=.e88b8993bfb1

CHAPTER TEN

Science Fiction and Fantasy: Going Where Few Blacks Have Gone Before

Representation can help us understand the world around us, particularly how and why it works the way it does (Hall, 1997). Media programs are specifically designed to represent our world. Orgad (2012) explains that media programs and products are constructed to produce meaning through representation.

> Representation refers to the process of representing, the process by which members of a culture use systems of signs to produce meaning. This highlights that representation is an active process of meaning production, the products of which are media representations, that is texts and images. (p. 17)

The constructionist approach to representation argues that selected depictions and specific meanings tend to become significant in society (Lacey, 2009). The production and consumption of media depictions, images and messages, involves the consistent negotiation of meaning. That negotiated meaning demarcates much of our experience and understanding of the world.

Silverstone (2007) defines representation as a site of power based on the symbolic production and reproduction of difference. Hall sees difference as binary oppositions. Binary oppositions are the way that words and images are used to play off of each other. For example, using opposing categories or ideas such as black/white or good/bad to classify or identify something. According to Hall, the impact of representations on societal structures marks a place where difference is used to explain things like normal/deviant or acceptable/unacceptable.

Brooks and Hebert (2006) discuss how the media has come to represent social reality. They explore race as a construct often created and changed to meet social, political, and economic needs in society.

> Working from it (race as social construct) compels us to understand the complex roles played by social institutions such as the media in shaping our increasingly gendered and racialized media culture. (p. 298)

As a matter of fact, Dill and Burgess (2012) suggest that social images have a persuasive power because they are a form of storytelling that can influence attitudes, feelings, and behavior towards others. The fact that the audience's reaction plays a significant part in the connection of race and representation is also acknowledged by Gray (2005) who believes that mediated images and messages when connected to cultural history and ideology can more easily resist stereotypes, particularly if you add levels of complexity.

> Historically black people in the United States have used the expressive arts and popular culture aggressively to imagine and narrate a collective past, the political aim of which was to protect black people, and that imagined past from the cultural control of whites. Expressive culture also provided a scene or space in which and from which to openly declare black anger and black beauty. (p. 121)

If representation becomes meaning, then to look at the representation of black culture in science fiction and fantasy is to look at the meaning of black culture as part of our imagined future. Hall, Evans, and Nixon (2013) proposes that representation involves the audience's mental assessment tied to a shared language. This system of representation they describe as a process used to understand the real and fictional world of objects, people or events.

For example, a report published in the *Fireside Fiction Magazine* found that only about two percent of the science fiction and fantasy writers who were published in the year 2015 were black. The editor of *Fireside Fiction* Brian White was not surprised (Flood, 2016).

> I think anyone who is paying attention to the demographics of speculative fiction publishing in general and short fiction in particular knows that there is a problem with the underrepresentation of people of color, and that it is even worse for black writers.

Nkadi (2017) in *The Root* asks, why is society intent on erasing black people in fantasy and sci-fi's imaginary worlds? There have been huge outcries against having a black Spiderman, Aquaman or the Human Torch, and even Idris Elba playing

Heimdall in *Thor* was criticized extensively (Dean, 2017). On the Harry Potter fandom website, J. K. Rowling includes a wizarding school in Africa, Uganda specifically, and this has been met with anger by some. It is said that African magic can heal a continent. It is spiritually rich with traditional beliefs, ancestral charms, and natural cures (Holland, 2003). Magic in Rowling's African wizardry school is based on the principles in astronomy, alchemy, and transfiguration (harrypotterfandom, 2019). Why is that a problem?

What better topic to end this exploration of racialism with than the examination of black representation in science fiction and fantasy. Growing up there was a joke in the black community about a conspiracy at work when it came to black characters in horror, science fiction and fantasy movies or television shows. Black characters were often the first to die. That is not the case anymore. In the twenty-first century it seems that things are changing, slowly.

Afrofuturism

Afrofuturism advances the future from a black perspective. In the early 1990s, Mark Dery used the term Afrofuturism to describe the exploration of black themes and the inclusion of black characters in movies, music, art and literature about the future (Dery, 1994). On a 2015 panel in New York City, Womack (2013) explains her vision of Afrofuturism as complicated.

> Afrofuturism offers a highly intersectional way of looking at possible futures or alternative realities through a black cultural lens. It is non-linear, fluid and feminist; it uses the black imagination to consider mysticism, metaphysics, identity and liberation; and despite offering black folks a way to see ourselves in a better future, Afrofuturism blends the future, the past and the present. (Thrasher, 2015)

According to Kilgore (2010), race must be a historically conceived component in the future of sci-fi and fantasy studies. He argues that race will continue to exist in our social and political lives therefore it remains crucial to the stories we tell.

> Perhaps the greatest challenge or potential of contemporary science fiction is to imagine political/social futures in which race does not simply wither away but is transformed, changing into something different and perhaps unexpected. This would require paying attention to an actual history of race (and racism) in which what constitutes the Other and the Self is always under revision (p. 17).

From a global perspective Afrofuturism is tied to folklore and cultural tradition. Samatar (2017) explains that the blending of faith and irreverence is key to a mixture of folklore and science fiction. Folktales, myths, and mysticism offer a broad opportunity to envision a future that does not look like the past when it comes to race and race relations. Harney and Moten's (2013) "double-capacity," Mbembe's (2007) "afropolitanism," along with Gilroy (2005) and Spivak's (2003) concept "planitarity" all offer alternative ways to view race, space and time in science fiction and fantasy. Space and time must be linked to the real issue of how race influences life in the future. Samatar suggests, "In the future—that is, in our time—things are different" (p. 176).

Speculative fiction should be saturated with issues of race as much as any other variety of popular culture (Carrington, 2016). In his book, Speculative Blackness: The Future of Race in Science Fiction, Carrington demonstrates the complex relationships that emerge when blackness is ultimately embraced as an important part of the future.

Science Fiction and Fantasy Exemplars

These are the facts: people of color will be the majority population in America by 2050 (*Progress 2050*, 2015) and the number of white (light skin) vs. black (dark skin) people around the world is about equal (Nybrink, 2017), so how can futuristic media products limit or eliminate people of color and specifically black people? According to a 2014 study, out of 100 top grossing science fiction and fantasy films only eight had a main character who was non-white and in six out of those eight movies the African American character was played by Will Smith (Barrett, 2018). Smith's science fiction and fantasy films have been huge hits like *Independence Day* (1996), *The Men in Black series* (1997, 2002, 2012), *I Robot* (2004), *I am Legend* (2007), *Hancock* (2008), *After Earth* (2013), and even more recently *Suicide Squad* (2016), *Bright* (2017), and *Gemini Man* (2019) so he deserves huge accolades.
But as representations evolve with an Afrofuturistic mantra we need to see more black survivors, black women heroes, black male champions and influential black cultural power. Below are a number of exemplars that are moving society in the right direction.

AVP: *Alien vs. Predator* (2004)

The science fiction film that took black survival to another level was *Alien vs. Predator*. Sanaa Lathan was the first black woman to secure the lead role in a science fiction film and she was the only member of the crew to make it out alive. Lathan played Alexa Woods the tour guide for an Antarctica expedition (Morales, 2004). After a satellite relayed a source of underground heat in Antarctica, the group gathered to investigate and they found a sacrificial chamber in a temple under the ice. What they don't know is that there are two alien species prepared to do battle down there. Several humans from the group are caught and used by the serpent aliens to create new fighters. Others find themselves caught in a maze and are killed by the predators.

Alexa is suddenly alone so she joins forces with one of the predators. Not only does she need his help, but if the predators are not successful in killing the aliens the earth could be destroyed. In the end, Alexa and the predator escape the underground cavern, but they are followed to the surface by the queen alien who kills the predator and is finally killed by Alexa. The predator's ship uncloaks and members of his culture retrieve the bodies of their dead. They honor Alexa by giving her the predator's spear. The only human survivor was the black woman!

Black Panther (2018)

Black Panther was not set in the future, but it confirms the future viability of African and African American culture. The representation of Africa as a continent with wealth and worth was new and exciting. It is the opposite of most messages received in the media concerning the motherland (Sy, 2017). Black Panther is a *Marvel Comics* superhero. The movie was written and directed by Ryan Coogler. It is based on the hidden nation of Wakanda where a vein of vibranium that came from space has enabled their society to advance in many areas like technology, health, and transportation while also maintaining their unique cultural traditions.

In a *Vox* article by Johnson (2018) called *Black Panther a celebration of black culture*, he explains that the movie celebrates everything from power and beauty to identity and pride.

> It's what's behind the lure of Wakanda, a land of black vibrancy, freedom, diversity, and discourse not blighted by outside forces or forced to negotiate with anyone but themselves. It's why the Killmonger/T'Challa chasm rings so true, as they both offer their own type of wish fulfillment for black viewers. Wouldn't it be nice to have a world where we aren't encumbered by systematic racism and oppression and are masters of our own destiny? And yet wouldn't it also be nice to galvanize a community with resources and political might to address and maybe even reverse the effects of systematic racism?

At a time when the American president makes crude remarks about shithole countries, Wakanda depicts the opposite concerning future possibilities. Smith (2019) maintains that this movie is central to understanding what it means to be black in America and in Africa.

After the Obama era, perhaps none of this should feel groundbreaking. But it does. In the midst of a regressive cultural and political moment fueled in part by the white-nativist movement, the very existence of *Black Panther* feels like resistance. Its themes challenge institutional bias, its characters take unsubtle digs at oppressors, and its narrative includes prismatic perspectives on black life and tradition.

The warrior women of Wakanda are a testament to the future of African culture as well. The Queen-mother, royal guards, and tech-genius younger sister present positive images of black women in an Afrofuturistic setting. The empowerment of black women comes full circle in *Black Panther*, along with the issue of black hair. From the queen to the warriors, from natural to bald, these black women define themselves as beautiful and strong and smart. Based on real history, King (2018) explains that the Dora Milaje female army was based on the Dahomey Amazons known as the only documented all female combat arm military unit in modern history. He adds, "In Wakanda, there are no women waiting to be saved. Instead they are the ones doing the saving." King also insists that *Black Panther's* formidable impact around the world is important because representation matters.

Black Novels

Black science fiction and fantasy authors like Octavia Butler, Nalo Hopkinson, Tanarive Due, and Steven Barnes have written stories surrounding black culture as a testament to the future and past. Steven Barnes (Barrett, 2018) expounds on Afrofuturism by asking "Who are we?" and "What is true about the world?"

An interesting household has to be the home of the husband and wife science fiction and fantasy duo Tanarive Due and Steven Barnes. Barnes has created upside down worlds where White Europeans are enslaved by Black Africans (*Zulu Heart*, 2018), where friendship overturns the misdeeds of evil, prejudice, and racism (*Lion's Blood*, 2011), and where invading armies are fought to preserve a magical mountain that has been home to many generations (*Great Sky Woman*, 2009). Barnes has also written science fiction and fantasy episodes for television shows like *The Outer Limits* (1995), *The Twilight Zone* (1959), and *Stargate SG-1* (1997) (Obenson, 2012). He and his wife Tananarive Due recently published a young adult novel together, *Devils Wake* (2012), placing people of color in the forefront of a mass zombie apocalypse.

Tananarive Due has imagined powerful tomorrows, yesterdays, and todays for black culture throughout her writing career. Her stories involve haunted houses tied to racial identity and voodoo (*The Good House*, 2004), a supernatural in-between world found in dreams (*The Between*, 1996), and an African Immortal series featuring beings who heal miraculously and live forever (*My Soul to Keep*, 1998; *My Soul to Take*, 2011; and *The Living Blood*, 2002). Her writing moves away from negative stereotypes and biased stigmas presenting more potent and interesting cultural representations.

Octavia Butlers' books explore humanity at different periods of time. In her *Patternist* Series, Butler takes the reader back to Ancient Egypt, then into the distant future. Throughout the series which includes, *Wild Seed* (2001), *Mind of My Mind* (1994), *and Patternmaster* (2014), one of the main characters Doro uses selective breeding to try and create someone like him, a telepath who lives forever. In *Dawn The Xenogensis Trilogy* (2012), after a nuclear catastrophe a black woman who has been orbiting the earth in a space ship for 250 years wakes up. And *Kindred* (2004) is a story about Dana, a free black woman who is sent back into slavery through time travel to help her ancestors (Heller, 2019). All of the black science fiction and fantasy books written by Butler are crafted through a cultural lens. Her work examines key societal issues such as slavery, morality, race relations, the clash between sexes, identity, fear, and discrimination.

Nalo Hopkinson places her fantasy black characters in the middle of Caribbean folklore. She helps us understand race though mystical narratives about, teenagers who don't fit in, women with the ability to find lost things, unfulfilled ghosts haunting a shopping mall, and men who are spiritually obsessed by greed. In an interview in *Wired*, Hopkinson admitted that the lack of representation for black people in science fiction and fantasy is troubling (Geeks Guide, 2013).

> So, the issues are still very, very much there, even though we talk about race a lot in literature, there's still this idea of, 'Well if we make this person blue and give them pointy ears, then we don't have to actually talk about what's happening in the real world.' And those of us who live in racialized bodies feel the lack, we feel that erasure.

Star Trek and Spinoffs Series (1966–)

Star Trek has been making cultural advancements in the area of Afrofuturism for many years. The first interracial kiss on television is claimed by *Star Trek* in an episode with Captain Kirk played by William Shatner and Lieutenant Uhura played by Nichelle Nichols. Nichols' character was the first black woman to have a co-starring role on a television show in 1968. She was the Communications Officer on the Enterprise. In "Plato's Stepchild", the storyline, shows aliens forcing Captain Kirk and Lt. Uhura to kiss. They try to resist but can't (Delmont, 2018).

Star Trek has been responsible for many spin-offs on television, in film, and even comic books with each new Star Trek product offering progressive, multicultural, and distinctive casts. *Star Trek: Voyager* (1995) introduced Captain Kathryn Janeway, the first female captain in space, Captain Benjamin Sisko was the first black Commander on *Star Trek: Deep Space Nine* (1993), and Commander Michael Burnham is the black woman in charge on *Star Trek: Discovery* (2017).

Captain Benjamin Sisco is introduced as a widow raising his son alone on the Deep Space Nine station. There is an immediate departure from the biased frame of black fathers who desert their children. Bastien (2018) writes that the representation of positive black fathers on television holds weight in our society. She explains how in the 1990s the relationships between Sisco and his son, as well as Sisco and his own father were important because those types of relationships between black men were rarely seen on television.

> Conversations about representation in pop culture often feel like too much of a numbers game. Whittling the value of a series down to who stars in and who creates these works can be useful when looking at the culture more broadly. But it doesn't tell us about the soul of the work, how it speaks to its audience, the history it reflects, the artistic risks it's willing to take in order to not only represent minorities, but to speak to their experience with care.

In one *Deep Space Nine* episode called "Far Beyond the Stars" Captain Sisco time travels back to Earth in the 1950s where he is no longer a star ship commander. Instead he is a magazine writer limited by his racial background. His memory has moved over into his imagination and his character Benny Russell has written a story about a black Starfleet captain that he wants to publish in a science fiction magazine. When Russell is not allowed to publish the article he eventually breaks down (Alexander, 2016).

> I am a human being dammit. You can deny me all you want but you cannot deny Ben Sisco. He exists! That future, that space station, all those people, they exist in here. In my mind where I created it. And every one of you know it. You read it. It's here.

Captain Sisco represents black identity and preserves his connection to black culture throughout the *Deep Space Nine* series. He talks about the history of black baseball, praises his father's Cajun cooking, explores certain events and people from Earth's black history, and brags about his African art collection. And later in the series, he also falls in love and marries Kasidy Yates, a black female freighter captain.

Black Lightning (2018)

Black Lightning, set in modern day, sends an important message about the need for black on black destruction to end. The character Black Lightning harnesses electrical power which gives him super human strength. He can also shoot electrical currents to stop his enemies. This show features a patriarchal family with superpowers who are fighting against real life and metaphorical problems in the black community such as drugs, guns, violence, gangs, racism, bad police officers, and corrupt government officials (Thompson, 2018). The father is Black Lightning and the oldest daughter is Thunder. Thunder is so strong she can create a sonic boom. The younger daughter's power is controlling fire. Finally, the mother is a doctor and she holds important knowledge about the influence of the green light drug which is responsible for the many powers among low-income community members.

The series starts out with Black Lightning working undercover as Jefferson Pierce, the principal of a prominently black charter high school, Garfield High. The older daughter works at the school while the younger daughter attends the school. The comic book environment for *Black lightning* is a normal city in America called Freeland, although metahumans exist they are not the real problem. The real problem is the 100 gang and a drug called green light, both are destroying the black community. Executive Producer Salim Akil (2018) wanted the series tied to reality addressing criminal justice and the need for change in the black community.

> Young people are being shot and people are going into churches, schools and movie theaters killing people. Gun violence in this country is real, and I didn't want to make it feel good when viewers watched it on the show. I didn't want the shooting of aliens or just faceless folks but people that viewers would become familiar with and begin to care about.

The need for a superhero to help with the problems in America's inner cities is not a bad idea for a fantasy series. Luke Cage as the protector of Harlem is another good example of a black superhero who fights to protect his community (Toliver, 2018). As a matter of fact, both Luke Cage and Black Lightning incorporate an authenticity that can go a long way in reaching black youth. Nama (2009) suggests that sci-fi is always dialoguing with the cultural politics of race in American society and there is no form of popular production that can stand outside of culture.

> Whether blackness in sci-fi cinema is now a symbol of sociopolitical solidarity that serves the cultural needs of a society in crisis or a meaningful indication that racial

inclusion is the normative convention of the present and the ideal condition imagined in the future, Hollywood sci-fi will point the way. (p. 165)

Black science fiction and fantasy is ever changing. Constructing and observing the future through a black lens could help society to better appreciate the evolution of blackness as a richly textured identity. A recent twist in the fantasy of *King Kong* on Broadway involves a major change where the woman who draws King Kong's attention is black rather than white (Sandoval, 2018). Sandoval explains that it is a musical starring, Christiani Pitts and a 2000 pound robotic puppet.

McDonald (2019) says the story of King Kong was birthed from white society's fears of black male sexuality victimizing white women. In this new version Kong is trapped, chained, and stolen from his homeland, brought by boat to a hostile world and owned by a white man who exploits him. Pitts character comes from a history of slavery so she tries to free Kong recognizing the similarities between them. According to McDonald the character moves away from being a victim, like the previous white women who played the role, instead she is an adventurous, independent, and determined black woman.

If you are a black author, producer, director, or actor what can you do when most representations suggest that the past is all about slavery and the future doesn't exist? You can change those representations.

References

After Earth. (2013). IMDb. Retrieved from https://www.imdb.com/title/tt1815862/
Akil, S. (2018). Interview in *The Undefeated*. Retrieved from http://theundefeated.com/features/behind-the-scenes-of-black-lightning-reveals-the-intersection-of-race-social-justice-and-culture/
Alexander, L. (2016). Far beyond the stars: The framing of blackness in *Star Trek: Deep Space Nine*. *Journal of Popular Film and Television, 44*(3), 150–158.
AVP: Alien vs. Predator. (2004). IMDb. Retrieved from https://www.imdb.com/title/tt0370263/plotsummary?ref_=tt_stry_pl
Barnes, S. (2003). *Zulu heart*. London, England: Aspect Publishers.
Barnes, S. (2009). *Great sky woman*. New York, NY: Del Ray Publishing.
Barnes, S. (2011). *Lion's blood*. London, England: Aspect Publishers.
Barrett, G. (2018, May 7). Afrofuturism: Why black science fiction can't be ignored. *BBC News*. Retrieved from https://www.bbc.com/news/newsbeat-43991078
Bastien, A. (2018, January 19). *Deep Space Nine* is TV's most revolutionary depiction of black fatherhood. *Vulture*. Retrieved from https://www.vulture.com/2018/01/deep-space-nine-revolutionary-depiction-of-black-fatherhood.html

Black Lightning. (2018–). IMDb. Retrieved from https://www.imdb.com/title/tt6045840/
Black Panther. (2018). IMDb. Retrieved from https://www.imdb.com/title/tt1825683/
Bright. (2017). IMDb. Retrieved from https://www.imdb.com/title/tt5519340/
Brooks, D., & Hebert, L. (2006). Gender, race and media representation. In B. J. Dow & J. T. Wood (Eds.), *The SAGE Handbook of Gender and Communication* (pp. 297–317). Thousand Oaks, CA: Sage.
Butler, O. (1994). *Mind of my mind.* New York, NY: Grand Central Publishing.
Butler, O. (1995). *Patternmaster.* London, England: Aspect Publishers.
Butler, O. (2001). *Wild Seed.* New York, NY: Grand Central Publishing.
Butler, O. (2004). *Kindred.* Boston, MA: Beacon Press.
Butler, O. (2012). *Dawn.* New York, NY: Open Road Media.
Carrington, A. (2016). *Speculative blackness: The future of race in science fiction.* Minneapolis: University of Minnesota Press.
Dean, C. (2017, August 21). 15 controversial superhero race changes that outraged fans. Retrieved from https://www.cbr.com/superhero-race-changes-in-film/
Delmont, M. (2018, September 5). Fifty years ago, *Star Trek* aired TV's first interracial kiss. *Smithsonion.com.* Retrieved from: https://www.smithsonianmag.com/arts-culture/fifty-years-ago-star-trek-aired-tvs-first-interracial-kiss-180970204/
Dery, M. (1994). *Flame wars: The discourse of cyberculture.* Durham, SC: Duke University Press.
Dill, K., & Burgess, M. (2012). Seeing is believing: Toward a theory of media imagery and social learning. In L. Schrum (Ed.), *The psychology of entertainment media: Blurring the lines between entertainment and persuasion.* New York, NY: Routledge.
Due, T. (1998). *My soul to keep.* New York, NY: Harper Voyager.
Due, T. (2002). *The living blood.* New York, NY: Washington Square Press.
Due, T. (2004). *The good house.* New York, NY: Washington Square Press.
Due, T. (2011a). *My soul to take.* New York, NY: Washington Square Press.
Due, T. (2011b). *The between.* New York, NY: Harper Torch Publishing.
Flood, A. (2016, August 9). Black science fiction writers face universal racism, study finds. *The Guardian.* Retrieved from https://www.theguardian.com/books/2016/aug/09/black-science-fiction-writers-universal-racism-study-finds-fireside-fiction-blackspecfic
Geeks Guide to the Galaxy. (2013, March 6). Nalo Hopkins new novels bring the mojo. *Wired.* Retrieved from https://www.wired.com/2013/03/geeks-guide-nalo-hopkinsons/
Gemini Man. (2019). IMDb. Retrieved from https://www.imdb.com/title/tt1025100/?ref_=fn_al_tt_1
Gilroy, P. (2005). *Postcolonial Melancholia.* New York, NY: Columbia University Press.
Goodwill, J. R., Anyiwo, N., Williams, E.-D. G., Johnson, N. C., Mattis, J. S., & Watkins, D. C. (2018, May 3). Media representations of popular culture figures and the construction of black masculinities. *Psychology of Men & Masculinity, 20*(3), 1–11.
Gray, H. (2005). *African Americans and the politics of representation.* Berkley: University of California Press.

Hall, S. (1997). *Representation: Cultural representations and signifying practices.* Thousand Oaks, CA: Sage.
Hall, S., Evans, J., & Nixon, S. (2013). *Representation.* Thousand Oaks, CA: Sage.
Hancock. (2008). IMDb. Retrieved from https://www.imdb.com/title/tt0448157/
Harney S., & Moten, F. (2013). The undercommons: Fugitive planning and black study. *Minor Compositions.* 101–159.
Harrypotter.fandom. (2019). Uagadou School of Magic Retrieved from https://harrypotter.fandom.com/wiki/Uagadou_School_of_Magic
Heller, S. (2019). Best Octavia E. Butler books. *Futurism.* Retrieved from https://futurism.media/best-octavia-e-butler-books
Holland, H. (2003). *African magic: Traditional ideas that heal a continent.* South Africa: Penguin.
I Am Legend. (2007). IMDb. Retrieved from https://www.imdb.com/title/tt0480249/
Independence Day. (1996). IMDb. Retrieved from https://www.imdb.com/title/tt0116629/
I Robot. (2004). IMDb. Retrieved from https://www.imdb.com/title/tt0343818/
Johnson, T. (2018, February 23). *Black Panther* is a gorgeous, groundbreaking celebration of black culture. *Vox.* Retrieved from: https://www.vox.com/culture/2018/2/23/17028826/black-panther-wakanda-culture-marvel
Kilgore, D. D. (2010, March). Difference engine: Aliens, robots and other racial matters in the history of science fiction. *Science Fiction Studies, 37*(1), 16–22.
King, O. (2018). The cultural impact of the *Black Panther* Movie on the African Diaspora. *Medium.com* Retrieved from https://medium.com/@olaking/the-cultural-impact-of-the-black-panther-movie-on-the-african-diaspora-1fdd329a8405
Lacey, N. (2009). *Image and representation: Key concepts in media studies.* New York, NY: St. Martins Press.
Mbembe, A. (2007). Afropolitanism. In C. Kellner & J. Media (Eds.), *Africa remix: Contemporary art of a continent* (pp. 26–30). London, England: Hayward Gallery.
McDonald, S. (2019, January 3). Can a black heroine fix the racist stereotypes infecting *King Kong? The Undefeated.* Retrieved from https://theundefeated.com/features/can-king-kong-racist-stereotypes-be-fixed-by-black-actress-christiani-pitts-in-fay-wray-role/
Men in Black. (1997). IMDb. Retrieved from https://www.imdb.com/title/tt0119654/
Men in Black II. (2002). IMDb. Retrieved from https://www.imdb.com/title/tt0120912/
Men in Black 3. (2012). IMDb. Retrieved from https://www.imdb.com/title/tt1409024/
Morales, W. (2004, August). *Alien Vs. Predator*: An Interview with Sanaa Lathan. *BlackFilm.com.* Retrieved from http://www.blackfilm.com/20040806/features/sanaalathan.shtml
Nama, A. (2009). R is for Race, not rocket: Black representation in American Science Fiction Cinema. *Quarterly Review of Film and Video, 26*(2), 155–166.
Nkadi, A. (2017, November 9). Why is society intent on erasing black people in fantasy and sci-fi's imaginary worlds? *The Root.* Retrieved from https://www.theroot.com/why-is-society-intent-on-erasing-black-people-in-fantas-1820214381

Nybrink, G. (2017, September 23). Are there more whites than black people in the world? *Quora*. Retrieved from https://www.quora.com/Are-there-more-whites-than-black-people-in-the-world

Obenson, T. (2012, August 9). Steven Barnes' *Zulu Heart* and other sci-fi, fantasy novels about black people in need of film adaptations. *Indiewire*. Retrieved from https://www.indiewire.com/2012/08/steven-barnes-zulu-heart-other-sci-fi-fantasy-novels-about-black-people-in-need-of-film-adaptations-143226/

Orgad, S. (2012). *Media representation and the global imagination*. Cambridge, MA: Polity Press.

The Outer Limits. (1995–2002). IMDb. Retrieved from https://www.imdb.com/title/tt0112111/

Progress 2050. (2015, August). Demographic growth of people of color. *Center for American Progress*. Retrieved from https://cdn.americanprogress.org/wp-content/uploads/2015/08/05075256/PeopleOfColor-Democracy-FS.pdf

Samatar, S. (2017, Winter). Toward a planetary history of Afrofuturism. *Research in African literatures, 48*(4), 175–191.

Sandoval, L. (2018). Christiani Pitts talks making history in King Kong musical as first black woman to play lead Ann Darrow. *Essence*. Retrieved from https://www.essence.com/celebrity/pretty-dope/christiani-pitts-talks-making-history-in-king-kong-musical-as-first-black-woman-to-play-lead-ann-darrow/

Silverstone, R. (2007). *Media and morality: On the rise of the mediapolis*. Cambridge, MA: Polity Press.

Smith, J. (2019). The revolutionary power of *Black Panther*. *Time Magazine*. Retrieved from http://time.com/black-panther/

Spivak, G. C. (2003). *Death of a Discipline*, New York, NY: Columbia University Press.

Stargate SG-1. (1997). IMDb. Retrieved from https://www.imdb.com/title/tt0118480/

Star Trek. (1966–1969). IMDB. Retrieved from https://www.imdb.com/title/tt0060028/

Star Trek: Deep Space Nine. (1993–1999). IMDb. Retrieved from https://www.imdb.com/title/tt0106145/

Star Trek: Discovery. (2017–). IMDb. Retrieved from https://www.imdb.com/title/tt5171438/

Star Trek: Voyager. (1995–2001). IMDb. Retrieved from https://www.imdb.com/title/tt0112178/

Suicide Squad. (2016). IMDb. Retrieved from https://www.imdb.com/title/tt1386697/

Sy, A. (2017, August 14). Exploring media sentiment around Africa: Positive or negative? *Brookings*. Retrieved from https://www.brookings.edu/blog/africa-in-focus/2017/08/14/exploring-media-sentiment-around-africa-positive-or-negative/

Thompson, G. (2018, January 11). Behind the scenes of Black Lightning reveals the intersection of race, social justice and culture. *The Undefeated*. Retrieved from http://theundefeated.com/features/behind-the-scenes-of-black-lightning-reveals-the-intersection-of-race-social-justice-and-culture/

Thrasher, S. (2015, December 7). Afrofuturism: Reimagining science and the future from a black perspective. *The Guardian*. Retrieved from https://www.theguardian.com/culture/2015/dec/07/afrofuturism-black-identity-future-science-technology

Toliver, S. (2018). Unlocking the Cage: Empowering literacy representations in *Netflix's Luke Cage* series. *Journal of Adolescent and Adult Literacy, 61*(6), 621–630.

The Twilight Zone. (1959–1964). IMDb. Retrieved from https://www.imdb.com/title/tt0052520/

Womack, Y. (2013, October 1). *Afrofuturism: The World of black sci-fi and fantasy culture.* Chicago, IL: Chicago Review Press.

About the Author

Venise Berry is an associate professor in Journalism and African American Studies at the University of Iowa in Iowa City. She received a BA (1977) in Journalism and an MA (1979) in Communication Studies from the University of Iowa. Her Ph.D. was awarded in 1989 in Radio. TV and Film at the University of Texas in Austin.

She is the author of three national bestselling novels, *So Good: An African American Love Story* (Dutton Penguin, 1996), *All of Me: A Voluptuous Tale* (Dutton Penguin, 2000), and *Colored Sugar Water* (Dutton Penguin, 2002). Her book of essays, *Driven: Reflections on Love, Career, and the Pursuit of Happiness* was published in 2018 by Jewell Jordan Publishers/BerryBooks. She is currently finishing her fourth novel *Pockets of Sanity*.

Berry is the co-editor of an anthology, also with Peter Lang, *Black Culture & Experience: Contemporary Issues* (2015) and co-author of two non-fiction film books, *The Historical Dictionary of African American Cinema* (Scarecrow Press, 2007 & 2nd Ed. 2015) and *The 50 Most Influential Black Films* (Citadel 2001). She has also published widely in other creative and academic circles with numerous short stories, journal articles, and book chapters. Her research focus is an exploration of media, African Americans and popular culture.

She was honored in 2018 with an Iowa History Makers Award from the African American Museum in Cedar Rapids, Iowa. In 2003, she received the

"Creative Contribution to Literature" award for *Colored Sugar Water* from the Zora Neale Hurston Society. *All of Me* received a 2001 Honor Book Award from the Black Caucus of the American Library Association. Her first co-edited anthology, *Mediated Messages and African-American Culture: Contemporary Issues* (Sage, 1996) won the Meyers Center Award for the Study of Human Rights in North America in 1997.

Berry serves on the faculty each winter in the Solstice low-residency creative writing program at Pine Manor College in Chestnut Hill, MA, and offers writing workshops each summer in the Iowa Summer Writing Festival. She has also conducted writing workshops with the Hurston/Wright Foundation and the Black Writers Conference and Reunion.

If you would like to bring Berry to your campus to teach a workshop or make a presentation contact her at: venise-berry@uiowa.edu For more information go to: www.veniseberry.com

Workshop/Presentation topics include:

- Racialism and the Media
- Weight and Wellness: Challenging Myths
- Success Strategies for the 21st Century
- Words That Set Us Free
- Food for the Spirit

Index

48 Hours 17
acting white 26
Affirmative Action 118–119, 128, 131
Affordable Care Act 134
Afrocentric 57
Afrofuturism 141, 144–145
Afropolitanism 142
After Earth 142
Aggression Theory 14
Alien vs. Predator 142–143
Amos, Diana 50
Amos and Andy 16
American Apparel 47
Another 48 Hours 17
Authenticity 30–31, 33, 36–37, 55–59, 64, 66–67, 101, 147

Bailey, Cynthia 27
Bamboozled 47
Barbie 45–46
Barnes, Steven 144
Barthes, Roland 43, 58
Bee, Samantha 87
Being Mary Jane 7

Benbow, Candice 117–118
Berry, Halle 75
Between, The 144
Beverly Hills Cop 17
Beyonce 47, 55, 117–118
 #LemonadeSyllabus 112, 117–118
biased framing 1, 3, 37, 43, 129–130, 133–135
 biased frames 4, 7–8, 32, 50–51, 56, 63–64, 127–135
Bible, The 85–86, 88–90, 131
Binary oppositions 139
Birther issue 130–132
Black American Princess 35
#BlackGirlMagic 112, 115–116
black identity 55–59, 66–67, 111, 143, 146
Black-ish 55–67
Black Jesus 87–96
Black Lightning 147–148
#BlackLivesMatter 111–114
Black Panther, The 1, 112, 114–115, 143–144
 #WakandaForever 112, 114–115
Black Pixies 20
Black Twitter 109–122

Bland, Sandra 113
Blaxploitation 17–18
Boondocks 86
Boughetto 28
Bourdieu, Pierre 109
Boyz N the Hood 34–35
Bright 142
Brown, Leroy 18
Brown, Michael 111, 113
Buckwheat 17
Bundchen, Gisele 1
Burris-Tucker, Kandi 27–28
Butler, Octavia 144–145

Campbell, Naomi 47
Capitalism 26, 33, 36, 90, 95
Cardi B 25
Caribbean folklore 145
Chance the Rapper 44
Chappelle, Dave 19–20
Cheerios Interracial ad 49
Chestnut, Morris 72, 78
Christianity 85
Chronic, The 33
Clark, Stephon 113
Clattenburg, Mike 85
Claws 25, 29
Clockers 34
CNN 29, 86, 115, 120
Cobert, Stephen 87
cognitive structural thinking 12, 20, 73
Cole, Robert Joe 2–3, 115
Colors 34
Colorism 47, 66
Coming to America 17–28
Commercialism 8, 33, 36
Commodification 8, 56, 67
Commodified 36, 57, 67
Common 56
conspicuous consumption 27, 36–37
conspiracy theories 131–132, 141
constructionist approach 139
consumption 13, 17, 27, 36–37, 112, 139
Coogler, Ryan 2–3, 115, 143
Cool Pose 16, 36

Cop Killer 33
COPS 72
Cosby Show, The 5
Crash 99–106
Criminal Minds 78
Critical Race Theory 5–6, 109
Cullors, Patrisse 113–114
Cultivation Theory 73
cultural capital 109–122

Dahomey Amazons 144
Daily Show, The 87
Daniels, Lee 28
Davis, Viola 74–75
Dawn, The Xenogensis Trilogy 145
Deadline Hollywood 85
Deconstruction 56–59, 64, 67, 101–102
Deconstruction Theory 58, 102
Dery, Mark 141
Devil's Wake 144
"differance" 58, 67
Discrimination 4, 6, 78, 104, 130, 145
Doggystyle 33
Dolemite 17
Double distinction 87
Dr. Dre 30, 33
Dreamgirls 17
Due, Tanarive 144–145
Duncan, Brandon 32–33
Duke, Winston 2–3
Dunkin Donuts 47–48

Elle Magazine 47, 71
Empire 28–29
Enemy Within, The 72, 78
Essence Magazine 115, 117
ethnic humor 13–14, 17–19, 21, 87

Fallon, Jimmy 87
Ferguson, Missouri 112–113
Fifth Element, The 19
Fisher, Abigail 118–119
free market capitalism 33
Fresh Prince, The 16
Freud, Sigmund 14

Friday 19
Foxx, Redd 16
F--- The Police 33
Fugate, James 29–30
Full Frontal 87

Gang Related 34–35
Gangsta rap 5, 33
Garner, Eric 113
Garza, Alicia 113
Gerber 49–50
Get Christie Love 73
Geto Boys 33
Ghetto 14, 16, 25–37
Ghettofabulous 25–37
Ghetto Nation 25–26
Good Form 34
Good House, The 144
Good Samaritan 89
Good Times 16
Gosden, Freeman 16
Gray, Freddy 113
Great Sky Woman 144
Grey's Anatomy 71, 76
Grio, The 119–120

Hancock 142
Hart, Kevin 18
Henson, Taraji 28
Hip Hop 27, 33, 50, 60, 105, 111, 119, 133
historical myths 1, 4, 7, 43–44, 51, 66, 129
Hobbes, Thomas 14
Hollywood 25, 100, 116, 148
hooks, bell 16, 31
Hopkinson, Nalo 144–145
How to get Away with Murder 71–72, 75–76
Hurricane Katrina 46
Hustle and Flow 26
Huxtables 5
Huxtable, Claire 75

I Am Legend 142
Ice Cube 18
Ice T 31, 33, 72, 77–78

#IfSlaveryWasAChoice 119–120
Independence Day 142
Interpretive communities 109–122
Intersectionality 99–106
I Robot 142

James, Lebron 1–3
Jay Z 133
Jesus 85–97
Joiner, Tom 86
Jumanji: Welcome to the Jungle 18
Juvenile 33

Kandi Coated Nights 28
Kaepernick, Colin 44
Kennedy, John 46
Kindred 145
Kingfish 16
King Kong 1–3, 148

Late Show, The 7
Lathan, Sanaa 142–143
Law and Order: SVU 72, 77
Leakes, NeNe 27
Lee, Spike 47, 116
Legend, John 56
Leibovitz, Annie 1–3
Lemon, Don 29, 86, 112, 120–121
    #DonLemonLogic 112, 120–121
Life cereal 49
Lil Jon 34
Lil Wayne 34
Limbaugh, Rush 121, 128, 132
Lion's Blood 144
Little Rascals 17
Living Blood, The 145
LL Cool J 72, 77
Los Angeles Lakers 1
Los Angeles riots 78
Los Angeles Times 116, 121
Lyons, Cookie 28–29

Mane, Gucci 33
Madea 7
majoritarian story 6

Malcolm X 46
Mann, David 8, 18
Marcille, Eva 27
Mars, Bruno 117
Martin, Trayvon 113
materialistic culture 31
McGruder, Aaron 85–86, 91, 97
McMillan, Terry 29
Meet the Browns 18
Men in Black 142
Menace II Society 34
Meyers, Seth 87
Minaj, Nicki 34
Mind of My Mind 145
Monae, Janelle 115
Moore, Kenya 27–28
Moore, Michael 116
Moore, Rudy Ray 17
Moore Shemar 72, 78
Moore, Tim 16
Murphy, Eddie 8, 17
Multidimensional 57
Multidimensional identity 101
My Soul to Keep 145
My Soul to Take 145

Noah, Trevor 87
NCIS: Los Angeles 72, 77
Nash, Niecy 25, 29
Nelly 26
New Jack City 34
New York Undercover 72
Nichols, Nichelle 145
Nigrescence 57
Nihilism 26, 33
Nivea 47
Nutty Professor, The 17
NWA 33
Nyongo, Lupita 47
NYPD Blue 72, 7

Obama, Barack 127–135
　Barack the Magic Negro 132
　Obamacare 133–134
Obama, Michelle 132–133
O'Reilly, Bill 128

#OscarsSoWhite 112
Outer Limits, The 112, 116–117

Pantene 48
Parody 85–88, 90–91
Patternmaster 145
Perry, Tyler 7, 18–19, 55
Pine Sol 50–51
Pinkett-Smith, Jada 116
Pizza Hut 45
Planitarity 142
politics of fear 7, 13, 65, 78, 113, 128, 132, 145, 148
polysemy 43
post modern 57, 67
post racial society 2
prejudice 4, 7, 103, 144
priming 7, 12, 129–130
Private Practice 71
Pryor, Richard 14

Racialism 1–9, 21, 30, 43, 47–48, 50–51, 56, 67, 78, 86, 106, 129, 141
racial macroaggressions 129–139
racial microaggressions 127–135
Racial Signifier 37, 43, 58, 60, 67
Racism 109, 20, 44, 78, 106, 127, 129–131, 135, 141, 143, 147
　Antiracism 100
　averse racism 4, 9
　colorblind racism 4–5, 9
　competitive racism 4
　enlightened racism 5, 9
　institutional racism 106, 127
　modern racism 4, 9, 20
　savvy racism 131
　systematic racism 6, 78, 129, 143
　subtle racism 4, 9
racist 1–4, 9, 11, 17, 20, 43, 47, 75, 100, 102–106, 117, 119, 129–143
rap music 5, 26, 27, 32–34, 44, 50–51, 60, 77, 133
Real Housewives of Atlanta, The 27–28
Real Husbands of Hollywood, The 18
Reign, April 116–117

Representation 2–3, 5–6, 16, 30–32, 49, 55, 58, 67, 72, 78–79, 86–88, 90, 92–93, 100, 102, 139–148
Rhimes, Shonda 55, 71–76
Rice, Tamir 113
Rich Niggaz 33
Ride Along 18
Ride Along 2 18
Rihanna 47
Rock, Chris 117, 133
Rush Hour 19
Rush Hour 2 20

Satire 19, 47, 86–88, 132
Saturday Night Live 17, 87
Scandal 71–73, 76
Selma 56
Semiotics 57–58
Sermon on the Mount 89
Singleton, John 35
Shatner, William 145
Showtime 17
Shrek 17
Sidibe, Gabourey 47
Situationism 110
Smith, Will 16, 116, 142
Snoop Dogg 33
Social Identity Theory 12–14, 56–57
Song of Solomon 88–89
Stargate SG 144
Star Trek 145–146
    Star Trek: Deep Space Nine 146
    Star Trek: Discovery 146
    Star Trek: Voyager 145
Station 19 71
#StayMadAbby 112, 118–119
Stepin Fetchit 16
Stereotypes 1, 3–4, 7, 11–21, 28–32, 36, 43–44, 50–51, 56, 60, 63–64, 66, 71–78, 86–88, 91, 104, 129, 131, 140, 145
    Angry Black Woman 71, 74–76
    Aunt Jemima 72
    Buck 72
    Coon 11, 15–20, 28, 72
    Jezebel 7, 71–72, 74–75, 118

Mammy 7, 50–51, 71–72, 74–76
Sambo 72
Sapphire 74
Uncle Tom 61, 72, 121
Zip Coon 11, 15–20
Street Lit 29–30
Structuralism 58
Suicide Squad 142
Superiority Theory 14
SWAT 72, 78

T.I. 33
Tometi, Opal 113
Thompson, CaShawn 115
Tonight Show, The 87
Top Conservatives on Twitter 111
TCOT 111
Townsend, Robert 35–36
Trading Places 17
Trump, Donald 65, 8, 119–120, 131–135
Trump, Donald Jr. 119
Tucker, Chris 8, 19
#TweetLikethe1600's 112, 119–120
Twilight Zone 144
Tyga 34

Union, Gabrielle 7
United Colors of Benetton 45
Urban Fiction 26, 29–30

Vogue Magazine 1–3

Waiting to Exhale 29
Walker, Jimmy 16
Washington, Kerry 73, 75
West, Cornel 9
West, Kanye 62, 114, 119–120
white supremacy 4
Whitfield, Shree 27
Wild Seed 145
Williams, Portia 27–28
Wright, Jeremiah Rev. 130–131

Zulu Heart 144

ROCHELLE BROCK & CYNTHIA DILLARD
Executive Editors

Black Studies and Critical Thinking is an interdisciplinary series which examines the intellectual traditions of and cultural contributions made by people of African descent throughout the world. Whether it is in literature, art, music, science, or academics, these contributions are vast and far-reaching. As we work to stretch the boundaries of knowledge and understanding of issues critical to the Black experience, this series offers a unique opportunity to study the social, economic, and political forces that have shaped the historic experience of Black America, and that continue to determine our future. Black Studies and Critical Thinking is positioned at the forefront of research on the Black experience, and is the source for dynamic, innovative, and creative exploration of the most vital issues facing African Americans. The series invites contributions from all disciplines but is specially suited for cultural studies, anthropology, history, sociology, literature, art, and music.

Subjects of interest include (but are not limited to):

- EDUCATION
- SOCIOLOGY
- HISTORY
- MEDIA/COMMUNICATION
- RELIGION/THEOLOGY
- WOMEN'S STUDIES

- POLICY STUDIES
- ADVERTISING
- AFRICAN AMERICAN STUDIES
- POLITICAL SCIENCE
- LGBT STUDIES

For additional information about this series or for the submission of manuscripts, please contact Dr. Brock (University of North Carolina at Greensboro) at r_brock@uncg.edu or Dr. Dillard (University of Georgia) at cdillard@uga.com.

To order other books in this series, please contact our Customer Service Department:

peterlang@presswarehouse.com (within the U.S.)
orders@peterlang.com (outside the U.S.)

Or browse online by series at www.peterlang.com.